The Airgun Shooting Handbook

Les Herridge

**Peter Andrew Publishing
Company Limited**

Copyright © Les Herridge 1994

All rights reserved

First published in 1994 by

PETER ANDREW PUBLISHING COMPANY LIMITED
4, Charlecot Road, Droitwich, Worcestershire, WR9 7RP

ISBN 0 946796 59 9

A CIP catalogue record for this book is available from the British Library

Typeset in Great Britain by
Peter Andrew Publishing Company Limited

Printed and bound in Great Britain

This book is sold subject to the condition that it shall not, by way of trade or otherwise, be lent, resold, hired out, or otherwise circulated without the publisher's consent, in any form of binding or cover other than in which it is published and without a similar condition including this condition being imposed on the subsequent publisher.

Contents

	Introduction					iv
	Acknowledgements	...	...	...	...	iv
1.	Plinking Good Fun	...	...	...	...	1
2.	The Field Target Shoot	...	...	...	...	8
3.	Vermin Control	...	...	...	...	23
4.	Mechanics of the Matter	...	...	...	...	40
5.	Accessories	...	...	...	...	54
6.	Refinishing and Customising	...	...	...	64
	Index	...	...	...	...	79

Introduction

My aim in writing this book has been to answer, in as straightforward a manner as possible, those questions which are commonly raised by newcomers to the sport of airgun shooting. I have tried to cover most aspects, from choosing a gun through to competitive shooting and vermin control. I have also outlined the importance of safety and of a mature approach to the sport.

Airgun shooting is a highly enjoyable and relatively inexpensive pastime which is available to a wide age group. It can provide many hours of pleasure and relaxation, and I hope that you will gain as much enjoyment from your shooting as I have done over the years.

Please always remember to act responsibly when you are dealing with guns and so help to maintain the high standards which are being established for this increasingly popular sport.

Acknowledgements

I would like to thank Ian Law for his valued assistance in the preparation of the sections relating to competitive shooting.

Chapter 1

Plinking Good Fun

Buy an airgun and you join many thousands of individuals who enjoy a satisfying and relatively inexpensive sport. Unlike many other sports it is possible to start very cheaply with a secondhand or budget airgun, plinking at improvised targets in the garden. If you intend to take up competitive shooting or become involved in vermin control you may need to spend a little more, but the choice is yours.

Selection of a suitable airgun is part of the enjoyment, but make sure you choose a weapon which is suited to the type of shooting which you intend to do. The companion volume to this book, 'Airgun Shooting – An Introduction', offers detailed advice on choosing an airgun, including information on the many different types available, but in general make sure that if you intend to hunt vermin you have a sufficiently powerful airgun to do the job. A field target weapon should be accurate and have adequate power to throw its pellets in as flat a trajectory as possible. An airgun intended for serious competitive target work needs to be able to cut it with the best, so expect to pay for the privilege.

For most newcomers to airgun shooting, backyard plinking forms their introduction to many pleasurable hours of shooting. This is an undemanding and casual form of the sport, with no rigid rules about what type of gun to use, what sort of sights it should have, how powerful it is, or any of the other requirements which competitive shooters consider important.

There is no doubt that some competitive marksmen take things altogether too seriously and end up losing sight of the sheer pleasure of shooting which is what attracted them to the sport in the first place. Plinking does not take itself at all seriously; it is all about having fun, and that is the reason it is so popular.

What exactly is plinking? The term is an American one which simply means casual shooting at improvised or random targets. The name probably came about from the sound that cans, a popular plinking target, make when they are hit. In its most basic form, plinking can simply mean going into the garden with your airgun and shooting the heads off a few dandelions growing in the lawn, or shooting flies off the wall of your garage. You don't necessarily have to plan a plinking session, you just find yourself with a spare half hour, take the gun and start shooting.

In common with any other branch of airgun shooting though, there is always something that can be done to improve the amount of enjoyment to be derived from plinking, and we shall look at these things.

First though, a word about safety. Airguns are potentially lethal weapons which are capable of inflicting severe injuries. People have died from wounds caused by airguns used carelessly in an unguarded moment. There is no need to become paranoid about the safety aspect, you simply need to be fully aware at all times that whenever the trigger of the gun is squeezed, either deliberately or accidentally, a pellet will leave the barrel and travel through the air until it hits something. That is a simple physical fact. If that something which it hits is a person, a domestic animal or a window, then you will be in serious trouble, and the consequences could be with you for the rest of your life.

The main thing is to ensure that pellets remain safely inside your garden when fired. If they go on to someone else's property then you are committing an offence if you have no permission to shoot over that property.

Similarly, you are not allowed to shoot in any public place, i.e., anywhere to which the public have free access, such as public footpaths, parks, canal towpaths and so on. So how can you make sure that pellets remain on your property and don't ricochet off as though they have a mind of their own? The answer can be summed up as follows:

(a) Know the law.

(b) Observe the safety code.

(c) Ensure your gun is well maintained and accurate.

(d) Ensure that you become competent in the use of the gun.

(e) Ensure that anyone else using your gun also complies with these requirements.

Plinking Good Fun

'Airgun Shooting – An Introduction', the companion volume to this book, expands considerably upon legal and safety matters and is useful for reference. Generally though, the application of normal common sense will ensure that your love of airgun shooting does not become a nightmare for others.

❑ Backstops

One of the problems with firing pellets at hard surfaces such as brickwork is that unless they strike at right angles to the surface they may easily ricochet in any direction. A pellet which has already hit a hard surface often has sharp or jagged edges, so if it hits somebody it may do more damage than a pellet fired direct. Always work out where a pellet is going to go *before* you squeeze the trigger. Is there a tree behind that dandelion? If so, is your gun powerful enough for the pellet to penetrate the tree

Have consideration for your neighbours or you may find yourself in trouble.

or will it bounce off at high velocity, perhaps making its way back to you with murderous intent? Remember too that what goes up most definitely comes back down. Don't shoot vaguely towards trees in the distance without knowing where the pellet may end up.

A backstop of some kind will prevent pellets from straying or ricocheting. All you need is something which will trap the pellets after they have hit the target, so that they expend their energy safely. Commercially made steel pellet traps are available or can be made, which trap pellets fired at card targets. You can make a cheaper backstop by filling a cardboard box with tightly packed folded newspapers or magazines. Turn the box around after a few hundred shots so as to present a new backstop face to which targets can be fixed.

Old carpets can make a good backstop, but they need to be thick, perhaps several layers; make sure that your gun is not so powerful that it simply shoots right through the carpet.

Brick walls can be an acceptable backstop but be cautious; if

A black circle painted on a cardboard box makes a simple yet effective target. The box is packed with newspapers to absorb the energy of the pellets harmlessly.

Plinking Good Fun

pellets do not strike at right angles they may ricochet.

Having set up a backstop, it is necessary to ensure that your gun can shoot straight enough not to miss the backstop altogether. For this you need to know how to zero your gun.

❏ Zeroing

Unless your gun has fully fixed sights, you will be able to adjust the point at which the pellets strike. You normally adjust only the backsight to do this, although on some types of gun you may have foresight adjustment as well. Telescopic sights usually have two removable caps which when unscrewed reveal screw adjusters for elevation (up and down) and windage (side to side) adjustment.

Set up a clean target card (don't use cans or other improvised targets) and arrange your shooting position so that you are able to support the gun without actually resting it directly on a hard surface as this is detrimental to accuracy. You may find that

A simple aperture rear sight.

carefully placed cushions may help. The idea is to ensure that you are as steady as you possibly can be when you shoot.

Fire 5 or 6 shots at the centre of the target from the distance at which you expect to be normally using the gun. Shoot at exactly the same point each time, i.e., the centre of the target, and don't be tempted to move the aim point to adjust for a shot that goes wide.

Observe where all the shots fell. If they are all over the place, check your gun for loose screws, leaking air seals or general wear. Alternatively, find a friend who is a steadier shot than you are to help with the zeroing.

Hopefully, all the shots will be in a fairly tight group at some point on the target. If they are not on the target, you will need to adjust the sights initially to simply hit the card and go from there.

Assuming the group of pellet holes is below and to the right of the centre, adjust the backsight *upwards* a little, and move it to the *left*. The simple rule to remember when adjusting open sights is to move the rearsight in the direction you want the pellets to go. The principle is exactly the same for telescopic sights, just use the 'up' and 'left' vernier adjusters.

It is as well to adjust just a little at a time to avoid over-correction of the error. Then shoot another course of shots and re-check. Repeat the process as necessary. Zeroing your own gun has the advantage that it compensates for your own eyesight and way of shooting, so if you shoot exactly the same way each time, your shots should go pretty much where you want them to go.

❏ Targets

The types of targets used by plinkers are legion and limited only by your imagination. Apart from conventional card targets, cards are available showing vermin species such as rats and pigeons. Part of the pleasure in plinking though is in using something less conventional to shoot at. Cans, matchsticks, used partypoppers, toy soldiers, plasticine, Plaster of Paris figures (mould your own), water filled balloons, fruit, vegetables, paintballs (from paintball guns), plastic bottles, clay pigeons (clay discs used as shotgun targets), used shotgun cartridges, film cartons, matchboxes, cigarette packets, Smartie boxes, sweets and dry lasagne sheets all make interesting targets which will keep you amused for hours. They may also give you hours of clearing up afterwards, so do your shooting in an area which is easily kept clean!

Some types of plastic can cause pellets to bounce off, especially if your gun is low powered, so if you have a low powered gun you may be wise to avoid using empty washing up liquid bottles and the like as targets.

Those with woodworking or metalworking skills may like to try their hand at building their own targets. Targets that do something other than simply fall down when hit are interesting. Set bells ringing or levers falling, or lights blinking if you have the ability to design such a target. You may even be able to sell the idea to a manufacturer if it works well.

❏ Games

Shooting in company with a friend allows you to play games while pinking. Again, your imagination is the only limiting factor. You could make up cards with segments marked off like a dartboard, with adjoining high and low score numbers, then play games based on dart scoring systems. You could each have a model army and take turns to shoot at the 'enemy'. Different figures would carry different scores. Use your guns to spell out words in pellet holes. The winner is first to guess the word.

Use your imagination and have fun plinking. Remember the safety rules though, especially if there are children about.

Chapter 2

The
Field Target Shoot

For many years, the only properly organised competitive airgun shooting to be found on any scale in Great Britain was in the indoor clubs and the pub bell target shoots. Anyone wanting to shoot in a match organised by an established airgun club was required to use only .177 calibre weapons, and to shoot at a fixed range of 6 yards or 10 metres, firing at card targets, unless shooting in the slightly less formal atmosphere of a bell target shoot.

Many airgun enthusiasts enjoyed the challenge of pitting their skill against others of similar ability, but found competitive target shooting a little restricting and lacking in variety. They tended, therefore, to compete with each other in small groups, often in the open air. They fired at the sort of targets which plinkers use every day – old cans, plasticine, toy soldiers and, of course, card targets like the match enthusiasts. They fired from a variety of different ranges, even trying long range shots to add interest to their sport and develop their skill.

There were those who felt that much outdoor shooting lacked the discipline imposed in formal target shooting. Yet many of these outdoor shooters believed that competitive airgun shooting could be very popular, if it were properly organised and if sensible safety rules were established to protect the public and those competing. They were proved right. Towards the end of the 1970s several field target competitions were set up under the sponsorship of one of the monthly airgun magazines, and under the watchful eye of several shooting organisations. With a shaky but enthusiastic start, organised competitive field target shooting had arrived. Of course, many clubs had already been field target shooting for some time, but now this branch of the sport really began to gain popularity on a national basis.

❏ Field Target Events

The major field target shooting events, which are generally held on a regular basis, are advertised in the airgun magazines and in local gun shops, and usually a telephone number is given for event enquiries. If you feel the need to write to the organisers, or if the shoot requires advance entries to be made by post, please help the organisers by enclosing a stamped addressed envelope. Entry fees are, on the whole, very reasonable, but if an organiser needs to reply to hundreds of applications, each requiring a stamp, then costs will escalate and this will obviously eventually need to be reflected in the entry fees to these events.

As with anything new, many first timers at a field target shoot

Associating with other enthusiasts allows the newcomer to try other types of airgun.

are a little nervous. If they are competing, the quality of their performance may be diminished by anxiety, and by being unsure of what to expect. It can be unnerving competing against a large number of people, especially if the individual has previously shot alone.

I have always been a believer in 'testing the water' before plunging in to anything new, so my advice to a newcomer would be to visit a field target event without taking a gun, and simply wander around, see what individual ranges are available, how registration is carried out, and what sort of targets you will be required to shoot at. Take a camera with you and act as an interested observer. Talk to the competitors and find out what they think are the likely problems for that particular day.

Perhaps there is a strong cross-wind, or maybe the course has been set up so that the competitors have the sun in their eyes for much of the day. Maybe the firing point is very muddy, preventing comfortable prone or seated shooting, or possibly an unexpectedly high turnout of competitors has led to long queues for certain events. This is, unfortunately, a common situation at field target shoots, and one which can allow nervous competitors to become rather uptight and consequently to shoot poorly when their turn does eventually come.

❏ Preparation for the Competition

When you are confident enough to take part in competitive field target shooting, the preparation for the event should take place over several weeks prior to the competition. You should be fully familiar with the gun which you intend using, and all your practice (and there should be plenty of it) should be carried out using only that particular gun. Select one brand of pellet which you know to suit your gun, remembering that accuracy counts for more than muzzle energy in a field target competition, then stick to using only that type of pellet. Use of a different pellet may require a change in the zeroing of the gun, so change should be avoided in the weeks leading up to a competition.

* **Checking performance of gun/sighting**

Obviously, any faults in the gun or its sighting system should be rectified well in advance of the event for which you are

The Field Target Shoot

preparing. Check that all screws are tight and that there is no obvious play in the action which should not be present. Any lubrication of the gun is best done several weeks before the shoot, as excess lubricant will cause an airgun to 'diesel', i.e., the lubricant will ignite under compression, in the same way as a diesel engine. If it is severe, dieselling causes erratic shots and can even permanently damage an airgun. The velocity of the pellet fired from an airgun which is dieselling badly will be in excess of the standard velocity, though it will not be consistent, and accuracy will suffer. Most airgun enthusiasts over-lubricate their guns anyway.

Modern weapons require very little attention – literally a few drops of lubricant every couple of tins of pellets is all that is needed, unless the manufacturer's instructions say otherwise.

The gun should be carefully zeroed some weeks before the shoot (see 'Airgun Shooting – An Introduction' for advice on zeroing), and if a telescopic sight is used – I would highly recommend that it is for a field target shoot – then it should be firmly mounted so that it cannot slide back in use.

* Practice

Practice, then, is the order of the day, or more appropriately weeks, since the more practice you have with your chosen weapon, the better your chances of making a good showing at the actual event. Remember, many of these field target competitions are won not by top names in airgun shooting but by unknown shooters.

Do not be intimidated by the presence of well-known and successful marksmen at the shoot. After all, the whole object of the exercise is really to have fun, and you are not likely to do so if you are tense and nervous. Try to relax, pretend that you are just plinking in the back garden at home, and do your best.

When practising for such an event, make a point of shooting at different distances from the target, learning instinctively how much holdover to allow on a long shot. Set up targets, at, say, five metre intervals, and include some very close ones. These can be among the most difficult to hit, until you realise that your sights are unreliable at close ranges. The barrel of the gun is, inevitably, a certain distance below the sights and, as a consequence, the pellet strikes lower than you might expect it to. You need to compensate for this factor, which varies from gun to gun, depending upon the sight mounts. Fire at least three shots at each target, so that the pattern is established, and the number of centimetres holdover, or perhaps holdunder, relevant for your particular airgun at a given range will become apparent.

The more powerful the gun, the less holdover is likely to be needed on distance shots, and this can be an advantage. The use of a .177 calibre air rifle can ensure a flatter trajectory, but a good .22 hunting air rifle should not need a lot of adjustment over the distances involved in a field target event, if the gun has previously been zeroed, for, say, 25 metres. One of the obvious attractions of field target shooting is that you are not, generally, restricted to any particular calibre in competitions. You are likely, however, to be required to have your air rifle tested on a chronoscope to ensure that the muzzle velocity is not above the legal limit. This test normally applies only to the main event at these shoots, and not to any side shoots.

It pays to arrive early at a field target competition to allow yourself time to become familiar with the layout of the ranges in use on that particular day. There is no set format, and the ranges tend to be organised to fit in with any natural features which may be present – a quarry or shrubbery, for instance. You will have time to gauge the effect of the weather on the shooting; it can be understandably difficult to concentrate with rain trickling relentlessly down your neck, and blustery conditions can play havoc with the scores too, as can unusually bright sunlight shining directly into your eyes.

* Clothing and equipment

Bearing in mind these last points, you will obviously need to come suitably dressed for the weather when competing in events such as this. Some form of hat with a peak is a must to shade the eyes and aid concentration. If the weather is likely to become wet, or is wet when you actually leave, a fully waterproof jacket will be needed. One that is merely showerproofed will soon let water through if it is exposed to continuous rain, even fairly light rain, for any length of time. The proofed cotton type of coat is to be recommended, although it can become extremely hot if the weather turns warm.

Suitable clothing should be worn underneath in case the coat needs to be taken off during the day. It is surprising how cold the hands can become on what may seem at first to be quite a mild day, so gloves may be useful. Personally I use thermal mitts, as these keep my hands warm, yet allow the use of fingers for loading the gun, handling pellets, and soon.

If you prefer to sit or lie prone when shooting, you may need to take a sheet of polythene or something similar with you, especially if conditions are likely to be muddy. You may find that waterproof overtrousers help you to be more comfortable when shooting in soggy conditions, bearing in mind that these shoots continue for most of the day, and even light rain will eventually find its way into your clothing if you are not suitably attired. You will find that field target shooters are a hardy bunch of people, and are unlikely to be deterred by rainy conditions. You can usually be sure that the event which you plan to attend will not be cancelled owing to bad weather, except, of course, in absolutely exceptional circumstances, in which case, a telephone call to the organisers will soon establish whether the shoot is to be abandoned.

You may find sunglasses a help in an outdoor shoot, but you may also find that they make it more difficult to see the detail on the targets. The painted metal type of target commonly in use soon becomes an even greyish colour all over, making it difficult to pick out the required point of aim. It is for this reason, too, that telescopic sights are more appropriate than open sights at field target shoots; they help the natural vision to pick out the detail on a target. Sunglasses, if used, should be of a type designed specially for shooters, without excessively dark lenses.

Ensure before you set off for the shoot that you have food with you for the day, and perhaps a hot drink, or soup, in a vacuum flask. If you are hungry, or otherwise uncomfortable, your shooting will not be up to top standard. Give careful thought before you leave to what you are likely to require on the day; the gun and a tin of pellets are by no means the only requirements. It is best to put together everything you need on the night before the shoot, so that you are not rushing around at the last minute, and perhaps becoming flustered because of something you are unable to locate or have forgotten to get.

* Registration, rules, safety

The first port of call on arrival at a field target competition must be the 'headquarters'. This is the registration office and is usually a tent or a caravan. Inside the office, the rules pertaining to the shoot will be prominently displayed, and these should be carefully read and understood before any shooting is carried out, regardless of how many other similar events you may have already attended. The rules vary only slightly from shoot to shoot, but some clubs often include a clause of their own; for example, one club may limit the number of attempts at any one event whereas another may allow any number of attempts at the same contest. It is best to read the small print.

Safety is always prominent in any rules at a field target shooting competition, and anyone who is not prepared to comply with the rules, or acts in a manner likely to endanger others, will be firmly asked to leave. This is important both from the safety viewpoint and from the public relations angle, as field target shoots are frequently held in country parks or other places where the public has general, and often unrestricted, access. Any bad behaviour, especially if it is seen to be accepted by the organisers, is likely to cause prejudice against airgun users.

If you make a point of arriving well before the start of the competition you will have plenty of time to acquaint yourself with all the relevant rules, and also have some time for a preliminary look around and perhaps a chat with some of the other competitors.

❏ The Different Ranges

A field target competition generally consists of a main shoot, usually set out in marked sections, or lanes, and any number of different side shoots, each offering variations of target and differing skill levels. There may also be a novelty shoot of some sort. A marshall is responsible for each section of the shoot, and he will look after you and instruct you in the requirements of his particular shoot as you reach the head of the queue. You should obtain a ticket from the registration office before setting off for the ranges, and this ticket should be presented to the range marshall as you start.

The Field Target Shoot

Let us assume that you are to shoot on the main course first. You will pay for your ticket at the office, then submit your rifle for chronoscope testing, which is often carried out in the same tent as is used for the office. Provided your rifle is safely within the legal limit of twelve foot pounds muzzle energy, you then walk out to the ranges to look for the zeroing range.

* **Zeroing range**

When an airgun is taken from one environment, a warm room for instance, into another, perhaps a cold windswept quarry where the shoot is being held, changes take place which can affect its performance – metal components contract or expand, altering working clearances; lubricants change in viscosity; condensation can form, etc. Consequently, shooters who have religiously zeroed their guns before setting out, and have checked that all is well, may find that accuracy is not what they expect once they reach the range. This is particularly noticeable when weather conditions are extreme, and some makes

Field target shoots are popular and usually well organised.

15

and models of airgun are more susceptible to these changes than others.

If a gun is not used for a while excess lubricant can build up, especially if it has been over-lubricated initially. The first two or three shots from a stored airgun are often unreliable, both in terms of accuracy and of power, and it is certainly necessary to fire one or two shots into the ground before starting to shoot in earnest.

To help counter these problems, a zeroing range is provided where competitors can check that their guns are performing effectively, and adjust them if they are not. This exercise allows the airgun to be warmed up and the firing clears the excess lubricant. The preliminary shots should be disregarded when using the zeroing range.

The zeroing targets themselves may be ordinary card targets or simple coloured discs on a white card. These are excellent as they stand out well even in poor light. Take care when setting them out that everyone has finished firing. The range marshall will let you know when it is safe to go down to the target area, and there may be some helpers who are prepared to set out zeroing targets for the competitors. Take your time when zeroing and be sure that everything is absolutely right before proceeding to the main range.

* **The main range**

The main range will have targets set out at various distances, from just a few metres to about 40 metres or more, and for convenience and ease of operation, as well as to save time, they are usually of the re-settable type.

The most popular type of field shooting target, and the one that has come to be accepted as the standard for the sport, is the silhouette of an animal or bird, e.g. a rat, rabbit, crow, or other generally accepted airgun quarry. This type of target is made of painted steel and has a circular cut out fitted with a disc. When this disc is hit, the whole target falls over and lies flat. If the pellet just hits the body of the target without striking the circle, which is about 2 inches in diameter, the target will not fall and the shot will not count as a hit.

The broad basis for this system is that the metal targets simulate animals you might normally hunt in the wild, and as a humane kill is essential, you obviously need to be capable of placing your shot very accurately. This type of field target enables you to judge your expertise very well. You can buy these targets yourself, too, if you have the space and would like to practise at home or on your own shoot. Once the circle has been hit and the target has fallen, signalling a hit, the device can be reset by the range marshall, usually by pulling on a string attached to the target, or by electronic means.

After a competitor has fired at all of the targets in the first lane of the main shoot, the marshall will mark the competitor's ticket, which doubles as a score card, to show the score achieved on that particular lane. The competitor then passes on to the next lane, where he is met by another range marshall, and repeats the process until he emerges at the other end with a completed score card and, hopefully, a good final score.

It may be necessary for you to shoot at a specified time on the main course, in which case you should present yourself to the lane marshall in good time to avoid delaying others. If you are late you may forfeit your chance to compete in the main event. In addition, you are more likely to be flustered, and possibly out of breath – hardly an appropriate state to be in when you are expected to shoot a few moments later. You may, of course, be one of those people who never becomes at all flustered. But for the rest of us, the advice must be to be prepared at all times. This applies both to the final moments before shooting and to the preparation for the shoot on the preceding evening.

When it comes to the actual shooting, take your time and direct your attention solely to the task in hand. This is often easier said than done, especially if you are unused to competing, but with a little practice, and allowing yourself time – reasonable time – to take each shot, it is possible to ignore much of what is taking place around you and to concentrate on your shooting. There are individuals who take far too long over their shots, holding up other competitors for an unreasonable amount of time. This is unfortunate, because not only does it upset other competitors, but it also encourages organisers to insist on time limits, and people often do not shoot as well if they know that there is a fixed restriction on their time. I should point out that I am only referring to extreme cases, so there is no need to be unduly concerned about the time you take.

Remember, though, that if you try and hold the sights on aim for too long there is a tendency for the gun to waver, especially if you are using a heavy hunting rifle. If you find this happens after aiming for a while, lower the rifle for a second then try again. Do not snap off the shot in the hope that it may be a good one.

I have seen competitors miss a shot after a run of success and then lose their concentration. In this respect the sport is much like any other, say tennis or golf, for example. Competitors blame themselves for missing what they consider a straightforward, perhaps even easy shot, and because they dwell upon what might have been, they fail to concentrate on successive shots properly. As a result, the final score is well down whereas it might have been one or two points below top score. The problem is understandable, but you should try to overcome this by treating each shot as the main shot. In other words, every shot you take should be treated as the only one you are going to shoot on that day. Forget those that have preceded it and those that will come later; give your full attention to the shot you are taking at any one particular time. It can be disheartening to miss two or three shots in a row, especially if your earlier performance has been exemplary, but everyone does it at some time or another, so avoid letting it affect the rest of your day's shooting.

* **Side shoots**

Apart from the main event, each field target competition has a number of side shoots. These vary in the skill level needed to compete successfully, and will often include some sort of novelty shoot.

The vermin range may be like a small version of the main range, with knock-down rats and rabbits peeping out from behind bushes and boulders. If the terrain is suitable, you may well be expected to climb into some awkward positions to take a shot, just as you would if you were hunting the real animals depicted by the targets. You may also be required to take the same target from more than one different position, to really test your skill in a simulated hunting situation. The targets will be set out at all the ranges at which you would be expected to shoot if you were actually hunting, with possibly an extra one or two placed out beyond the normal range to add an additional challenge.

Scoring is usually similar to the main event, with a fixed number of targets being shot. Side shoots may or may not carry prizes; some are provided for entertainment only, and to help reduce the strain of numbers competing at one time in the main event.

* **Novelty shoots**

There may be a rare chance to fire a collector's airgun, such as the long lasting and still much used Lincoln Jeffries rifles, or perhaps early Webley rifles which were so well made that many are still in regular service to this day. Since it is not usually possible to try these old guns beforehand, success is literally a hit or miss affair, but it is always valuable and enlightening to be able to try as many different airguns as possible.

Be careful when using these old timers though. For obvious

There may be a rare chance to fire a collector's airgun at one of the side shoots.

You often have the chance to try out rare or unusual airguns.

reasons they are irreplaceable, so handle them with the respect they deserve, even if they do look worn and tatty.

* **Pistol range**

You may like to try your hand at the pistol range. One of these is often provided, and you may find yourself shooting at card targets, at clay pigeons (discs of clay which shatter satisfyingly when hit), or even at tin cans. You may use your own pistol for this event, but one is normally provided for those who have only brought rifles but would like to try their hand at pistol shooting. This range may just be for fun or it may be possible to score and win a prize.

Not many airgun shooters are proficient with a pistol so, if you have any sort of aptitude for air pistol shooting, you might find this well worth a try. 'Scopes may be permitted here.

* **Hidden target shoot**

There is a course which has been used with success at some shoots, and that is the 'hidden target' shoot. In this competition, targets are concealed at various points in the course, and competitors, accompanied by a range marshall, are required to find as many of the hidden targets as possible and to shoot at

The Field Target Shoot

them.

The number of targets hidden will not be made known before the shoot, so to pick up the maximum number of points available the competitor must rely heavily upon his own powers of observation, something he would need to do for successful hunting.

Naturally, a varied terrain with plenty of natural cover is more appropriate for this type of shoot, because it is difficult to conceal targets on a closely cropped, flat grass meadow.

To make life a little harder still, there is usually a time limit placed upon the hidden target shoot.

* Snap shooting range

One of my own favourite field target ranges is the snap shooting. It may go by other names, but is basically the same as the army snap shoots, where the competitor fires at a target, often the silhouette of a soldier, which only appears for a few seconds. The target is electronically operated, and lies flat for a measured number of seconds while the airgun is being loaded and cocked. It then stands up for several seconds while the shot is taken, and then lies flat again for re-loading for the next shot. The duration of the rest period and the shooting time available can be controlled by the operator.

The competitor may be required to take five shots in succession to score, and this range is a good test of reflexes. It is easy to be caught out by the target popping up before loading is completed. This necessitates a very hurried shot before the target disappears again, and the rhythm of shooting is upset, with detrimental results to the score.

Rhythm really is the key to success in snap shooting, with a smooth cocking and loading movement being followed up by a relatively unhurried shot which is let off a second or so before the target is due to drop back down.

It may pay to count off the seconds as other competitors are shooting, so that you have a reasonable idea of when the target is going to come up or fall back down.

This is quite challenging shooting, and it is all too easy to drop a pellet while fumbling with the mechanism. Logically, then, all pellets should be readily to hand, and the shooter should be comfortably settled before starting.

There are only three types of airgun suited to this type of shooting: break barrel rifles, which can be cocked and loaded quickly; repeating types which feed the pellet in automatically as the weapon is cocked; and those which use a pre-charged system.

A variation on target snap shooting of the type described may be seen occasionally. That is a combination of the hidden target and the snap target, where targets pop up in unexpected places and remain for a few seconds before disappearing again. These electronically controlled targets are naturally expensive, and smaller clubs are unlikely to be able to afford to use them.

* **Decoy pigeons**

Heavy pellets are preferred for these plastic pigeons.

The number and variety of available side shoots at a field target competition is limited only by the imagination of the organisers and by the restrictions of the site chosen for the event. Some clubs are more inventive than others, some obviously have less money to spend and other clubs may have difficulty in obtaining a suitable site.

There is evidence that field target shooting is growing in respectability as it grows in popularity. Enthusiasts should support these events to show the public that airgun users are participants in a legitimate sport, and in pursuing that sport are able and indeed anxious to be seen acting in a responsible manner at all times.

Chapter 3

Vermin Control

The motivation to hunt is not altogether clear cut. It may well be a combination of things: the farmer may hunt to control a particular vermin species, perhaps wood pigeons which are ravaging his crops. Another individual, bored with pre-packed supermarket food, may really relish the thought of a fresh rabbit for the table, knowing that his dinner will not have lain in a deep freeze for months on end before being prepared.

Undoubtedly, the motive which provokes most controversy is that of hunting for sport, that is to say, hunting for the enjoyment of pitting one's wits against those of a wild animal. Man is, by nature, a predator, dominating animals to a greater or lesser degree, and the urge to hunt probably goes back many years to when man had to hunt to survive.

Those embarking on a hunt should remember that anyone who goes into the countryside and wilfully shoots at anything and everything that moves is both irresponsible and destructive. Such action quite rightly invokes public concern, and can do great harm to the image of airgun shooting as a sport.

Conservationists care deeply about the countryside and the preservation of wildlife, though it is not always understood that hunters themselves must also be conservationists. Obviously, there is no merit in killing off all the rabbits in an area. A shoot, as hunting land is termed, must be well managed and farmed to achieve a proper balance. This is the essence of good husbandry, and the basis of sensible hunting.

Assuming you have been successful in finding a shoot, the next task is to acquaint yourself with the terrain. Do not even consider shooting until you have first walked around every inch of the land *without* a gun. Observe and commit to memory every aspect of the ground, noting where wild creatures have been, or are likely to be, and recording areas of cover which may come in useful later.

❑ Fieldcraft

As you do this, you will become aware that fieldcraft is a primary element of a successful hunt. You are not likely to be very successful unless you learn the ways of your quarry: its habits, what it likes to eat, how it detects and signals danger, what signs it leaves of its passing, etc. Carry fieldcraft to the ultimate conclusion and you will develop a deep affinity with nature, with a feeling of actually being an integral part of the natural world, like the people who work in the country all the time.

You need to be very much aware of your surroundings: avoid stepping on dry, noisy twigs, stay downwind of the quarry so that your scent is carried away from, and not towards, the animal. You may not think that you smell particularly strongly, but it might surprise you to know that a great number of animals are capable of detecting your presence from well over 100 metres away, if the wind is blowing from your direction to them; a thought well worth reflecting upon when you are stalking.

Most of all, though, patience is called for when embarking upon a hunt; if you are the impatient type, then hunting is definitely not for you. To be successful may entail sitting or lying motionless for an hour or more in an awkward position. Merely strolling around the countryside in the hope of finding something to shoot at is not just irresponsible, but is almost certainly doomed to failure. Develop proper fieldcraft skills, avoid shooting at everything that moves, and you will find that you become so engrossed in your surroundings that you have no time to be bored.

Part of the attraction of hunting must certainly lie in the skills involved in competing with nature, in pitting one's wits against creatures which have had to develop the art of survival to a fine degree.

I do a fair amount of my hunting with a camera and, though I would not have believed it possible when I was younger, I gain as much enjoyment from 'shooting' with a 35mm camera as with something more lethal. Apart from the actual shot itself, be it from airgun or camera, the rest of the hunt is virtually identical: the study of the terrain in advance for evidence of the quarry which is being sought; the preparation for the hunt

Vermin Control

(including the selection of appropriate equipment and camouflaged clothing, to ensure that the hunter blends in with the countryside); the detailed search for the quarry itself; the stalk (which may involve an hour or more of messy, uncomfortable crawling through brambles, ditches, and across sharp stones, possibly in pouring rain); and, finally, the 'kill'.

When a hunt has been approached methodically, with much preparation and observation, the eventual point when the trigger of the gun is squeezed is almost an anti-climax, signalling as it does the end of a whole series of enjoyable events.

❏ Types of Vermin

The question of what to hunt should be of concern to anyone contemplating the pursuit of living creatures with any sort of weapon. Generally speaking, a creature which is regarded as a threat to the well- being of man for any reason is regarded as vermin, and as such considered fair game for the hunter. It may qualify as vermin by virtue of its taste for farm crops, or perhaps by its habit of creating dangerous burrows into which unsuspecting farm animals may stumble and be injured. It may block chimneys by building nests in awkward places, or steal the eggs and young of protected species of birds. It may damage young trees, and thus gain unpopularity with forestry workers. It may be a carrier of disease, contaminating stored feedstocks or destroying valuable crops or equipment.

Yet the fact that an animal or bird has been known to do any of these things does not necessarily mean it is classed as vermin, or that it should be relentlessly pursued as such. National law on the subject is not always clear or correctly interpreted, and local byelaws may exist which are relevant: an animal or bird which is regarded as vermin in one part of the country may not necessarily be viewed in the same way elsewhere. Sometimes farmers or ill-informed gamekeepers break the law by shooting protected species, such as birds of prey in the belief that those birds are vermin. Certainly, it is easy to see that birds of prey in any numbers could pose a threat to a well-run pheasant shoot, and as such might qualify for the 'vermin' tag, as far as the gamekeeper is concerned. As an intending hunter, you must consider that it is the law, not individual opinion, which lays down specifically what you may

The Airgun Shooting Handbook

or may not hunt, even if that law may be interpreted differently from region to region. There have been cases where creatures generally considered to be vermin have been shot by airgun users and the action has resulted in a charge being brought by the local police (often in response to a complaint from a member of the public), and a fine from the magistrates has been known to follow.

The status of some species of vermin may even change depending on the time of day! The humble rabbit becomes, for the purposes of the law, 'game' under certain circumstances – after nightfall, for instance – and an offence may be committed when these animals are hunted after dusk, unless certain conditions are observed.

It will be clear, therefore, that a careful investigation of how the law is interpreted and operated in your own particular area is essential before embarking upon a hunting expedition. Bear in mind, too, that most wild birds are protected by law, and

Have respect for wildlife.

apart from a fine, anyone killing or injuring a protected species can expect to have his gun confiscated.

Generally speaking though, provided that you have the necessary permission to shoot; rats, rabbits, grey squirrels, wood pigeons and many members of the Corvine (crow) family will normally form the vermin hunter's quarry. All can be extremely destructive and their control is vital to good farm management.

This list is not exhaustive, nor is it intended to be, but if you are tempted to shoot at anything which is not on the list, be absolutely certain that it is not a protected species. Wildlife is not provided simply for hunters' pleasure, and we have hopefully progressed since Victorian times when so-called sportsmen would decimate wildlife indiscriminately. Be a conservationist and help to protect what is left to us. Remember, your future pleasure and that of your children depends upon an enlightened attitude to the countryside and to its wildlife.

❏ Where to hunt

If your neighbour objects to you hunting, even on your own land, there is a provision in law for you to be brought to account if it can be shown that a nuisance or danger to the public has been caused. Always exercise great care when shooting, and make enquiries with your local police force before setting off on a hunt. Make sure that you obtain the name of whichever officer advises you, in case of future reference.

Over the years, as a result of their destructive antics with airguns, some irresponsible individuals have succeeded in attracting the adverse attention of the press. The mention of airguns and hunting in the same sentence will usually result in instant criticism. Yet the right airgun, used at a sensible range by a marksman who has taken the trouble to ensure that his shooting is of a high standard before embarking upon a hunt, can be more humane than a shotgun, which, with its tiny pellets, can often fail to achieve a quick, clean kill, unless range and judgement of the shot are exactly right. The shotgun has attained a lofty position of respectability, while the airgun has achieved relatively little general acceptability within the hunting field, though it is widely respected as a target weapon. The reason for this is, I believe, guilt by association, with the public at large tending to link the airgun with the vandals who sometimes use them. This is, perhaps, somewhat unfair logic, since shotguns do not generally attract the blame when they are used in armed robbery.

It is not universally known, but there is little, if any, variation in effective range between a twelve bore shotgun and an air rifle with a muzzle energy near the legal limit. This fact has a little more to do with accuracy than velocity, though, since with a shotgun the 'holes' between the shots become larger as the shot travels further from the barrel. It means that at extreme ranges, unless the shot misses the target completely, it is likely that only a single small shot may strike home, having perhaps insufficient energy for a clean kill by itself.

A good quality, well-maintained, high powered air rifle may be justifiably regarded as a viable alternative to a shotgun, then, for vermin control purposes. If in doubt as to whether your own airgun is up to standard for vermin control, seek advice from your local gun shop, which may have facilities for your gun to be velocity tested on the premises – a facility which is becoming increasingly common.

It is important for anyone intending to go hunting to ensure that the standard of their shooting is sufficiently high to guarantee that the pellets reach the intended target. A fast and humane despatch should be the goal of every conscientious hunter, and this can only be achieved if the hunter practises constantly.

Practice should involve shooting at a variety of different targets of varying shape and size, and at different ranges and angles of fire. If possible, take your targets out to the shoot and set them up in areas where you might expect to find the vermin you intend to hunt. You can then shoot from the sort of angles and distances that you might expect to encounter when actually engaged in the hunt.

It will be of help to you to attend some field target shoots, too (see Chapter 2). These offer the sort of varied open air target shooting which comes nearest to simulating conditions you may encounter in the hunt. You will find that if you do not practice for a week or so, your shooting may not be as good as you had expected. Constant practice is essential if you intend to hunt humanely.

Farmland is the logical place to seek to hunt vermin, and if you know a landowner who will allow you to shoot over his land then

Vermin Control

you are fortunate. If not, you could check advertisements in the airgun magazines which are published monthly, or put in an ad. yourself.

The best method of finding a shoot though is to knock on doors. Identify a number of potential sites where perhaps you happen to know that pigeons or rabbits are eating crops, and call to talk to the farmer to offer help.

Be prepared for refusals as landowners are often understandably wary of strangers. You may like to offer your labour to help around the farm, or perhaps a cash payment in exchange for being permitted to shoot: don't expect something for nothing.

The way in which you approach landowners will determine how successful you are. Arrive in full camouflage gear, armed to the teeth, and you will be promptly shown the door. Far better to dress respectably, call without your gun, and avoid disturbing people when they are clearly busy.

A brief, well-written and polite letter may achieve a positive response. You could follow up the letter with a visit after a reasonable interval. Explain clearly exactly what your intentions are and offer reassurances that you are a responsible individual who will not leave gates open or place any risk upon farm animals. Should you subsequently betray the landowner's trust, you will lose the shoot for yourself and any future hunters.

Owners of disused buildings may allow you to control rats, but beware of decaying buildings which may be structurally unsafe. Vermin control is sometimes permitted at privately run refuse tips, but local authorities are less likely to grant such permission, but there is no harm in asking. Do it by letter though, and be prepared for a long wait for an answer.

Do not hunt on so-called 'Common land' or anywhere the public are permitted to go, such as public footpaths, canal towpaths or parks. To use a gun in such places is a criminal offence unless you have been authorised by a local authority for instance to carry out vermin control.

There is really no such thing as land which is not owned by somebody in Britain. Land may be derelict, badly managed or totally neglected, but you must still obtain permission before you shoot there. You could otherwise be charged with armed trespass and other offences. Your gun could be confiscated.

❏ How to hunt

Having established what and where to hunt, it is next necessary to give thought to how. We have already seen that careful observation and preparation are needed when about to hunt, and that good field craft is a prerequisite for the successful hunter. In addition to general field craft, it will be essential to learn as much as possible about the habits of the individual vermin species being hunted. Where do they feed? What routes do they take to reach those feeding places? Are they exceptionally shy, or are they fairly used to people passing?

If you are hoping that your hunting will help the farmer who works the land over which you will be shooting, you have an additional avenue of approach. Any farmer who is having trouble with vermin, whether they are ravaging his crops or devastating his stored grain, will be sure to know where to look to find those vermin, and what their habits are. After all, he works the land every day and knows every inch of it, so a fact-finding conversation with the farmer before you start could be worth days of personal observation of the shoot. Do not be afraid to accept advice, because even if you spend all your life hunting, you will never learn all there is to know about the subject.

* **Hides and camouflage**

If it is your intention to shoot over one particular patch of land on a regular basis, it may be worth your while erecting a hide. This has a number of advantages. Provided the owner of the land has no objections to the erection of such a structure, a hide can provide the hunter with a relatively comfortable resting place while awaiting the arrival of the vermin, and can even be equipped with a waterproof roof if desired.

By virtue of its name, the function of a hide is to provide concealment for the hunter. However, it need not necessarily be camouflaged, because wildlife quickly becomes used to new structures, such as small sheds or stables, and tends either to ignore them completely after a few days or else use them as perching places.

The simplest form of hide is made by using the natural cover offered by existing bushes or thicket, and perhaps adding a few leafy branches to complete it. A bale of hay or straw makes a good seat, and could, if you wish, be used to construct a complete hide – especially useful in an area where there is little natural cover. A piece of old corrugated iron, perhaps covered with leafy branches would make a good roof.

There is really no limit to the variety of materials or different designs which may be used to construct a hide, although I feel that it is a challenge to be able to create one out of natural foliage wherever possible. That has the additional advantage of being less noticeable than a structure fabricated from man-made materials.

Remember to site your hide with regard to where you expect to find the quarry you seek, so obviously the preliminary reconnaissance is doubly essential here, especially if the hide is to be permanent. Ensure, too, that you have allowed yourself a wide field of fire from all angles without sacrificing concealment.

Try to view the scene as visualised by your quarry, and it will do much to help you be a more effective hunter. For instance, a wood pigeon homing in on a farmer's crop of brassicas would expect to see a quiet countryside scene with no visible humans close by, and nothing to deter it from its planned feast as it approaches.

Imagine, then, as it flies in for its meal over what it takes to be a stack of hay bales, it suddenly spots a pale blob moving about among the bales. Sensing that something is out of place with the scene, it quickly veers off and flies away in alarm.

The blob was the poorly concealed face of the hunter, and if you do not believe that a wood pigeon is capable of spotting a man's face from a long way away, then I suggest you put it to the test some time and prove to yourself just how uncannily observant these birds are. Much the same applies to other vermin, whose lives depend on their ability to detect and avoid trouble every day of their lives.

So the lesson is 'do not underestimate your quarry'. Camouflage clothing can obviously be of help when hunting – a bright shirt and fashionable trousers may look very fetching at the disco or as you stroll along the seafront, but the only wildlife which is likely to come anywhere near you if you wear the same gear on a hunting trip will be mosquitoes and wasps. Sober, even drab clothing blends in better with the surroundings in the countryside.

There is no need to spend a lot of money on camouflage equipment, unless of course you want to do so and have the cash to spare. An old shirt or jumper of a dull brown or green shade will help to ensure that you blend in with, rather than stand out from, the countryside. Match this with dark trousers and a hat of a similar shade, with maybe a peak to cover your eyes against the sun and shield your face from above. Add a pair of stout walking boots and you are in business.

It takes some nerve, but if you do not mind spreading stage make up or even mud over your face and the backs of your hands, and ignoring the fascinated or nervous stares of passers-by, the improvement in your hunting success rate may prove the exercise to be worthwhile. Of course, if your skin is already of a suitably dark hue then you have a built-in advantage.

Avoid taking out a white handkerchief when hunting – at least when you are in full view, as it will frighten away everything for miles around. Smokers will probably find it to their advantage to become non-smokers during a hunt because the smell of tobacco is very lingering and may well give away your position needlessly. Even with my relatively poor sense of smell, I can detect a smoker from hundreds of metres away when I am out shooting, so for any creature with a better sense of smell than humans, and that includes just about every vermin species apart from birds, the smell must be overpowering. That is not to say that smokers are necessarily unsuccessful hunters – if farmworkers regularly smoke in the area, the animals may have become used to the smell and it will not cause any alarm.

* **Calibre**

After weighing up the advantages and disadvantages of the available calibres it then falls to the individual to make a decision upon which calibre to use. Obviously, this is a decision which must be made when an airgun is purchased. If hunting is your likely goal, you must buy a gun in the calibre you deem to be appropriate, and of the specification which will do the job efficiently and be comfortable for you to use all day without exhausting you, either by its weight or by its poor balance.

Ignoring the few lesser known calibres such as .20 and .25,

Vermin Control

the main choice is between .177 and .22. These measurements are in inches.

The companion volume to this, entitled 'Airgun Shooting – An Introduction', examines in some detail the arguments for and against each calibre, but put briefly, the smaller .177 pellet has a flatter trajectory. This means that for a given power level, the pellet will not fall too quickly off target at longer ranges. Therefore the airgun can be zeroed for say 20 metres and still be within perhaps half an inch up and down of the target at 10 metres or 30 metres. This feature has made the calibre popular with field target shooters, but obviously the power of the gun is a major factor.

.22 has traditionally been the calibre for hunting on the basis that the larger pellet delivers more energy to the target, ensuring a quick kill. This principle is derived from firearm ballistic tests and holds less true for air powered weapons, though it is still broadly correct.

Provided the vermin hunter aims for a sure kill zone such as the head, the question of calibre is to some extent academic. because both .177 and .22 will do the job provided the gun is sufficiently powerful. Since this is the ideal, then calibre should be relatively unimportant. In practice. where the hunter's skills are a little less than ideal, observation has led me to the conclusion that .22 is a little more likely to kill cleanly than the .177, but it must be said that the difference is probably marginal. In the end it comes down to personal preference.

Experimentation will eventually lead you to favour one calibre over another. Once you have made your choice, stick with it and become proficient.

* **Pellets**

In hunting, much the same rules apply to pellets as they do to competitive target shooting, or to any other kind of shooting for that matter. Find out what types of pellet suit your own particular gun and stick to them. By all means allow yourself to be wooed by the enticing claims of the advertisers for the latest line in hunting pellets – that is part of the enjoyment of the sport – but do all your testing and evaluating in the garden and on the practice range before venturing out on a hunt. You owe it to whatever you are hunting to shoot to the highest possible standard, and pellets are very much a part of that search for perfection.

Should you take a companion with you when you hunt? There are advantages and disadvantages in doing so, and it is worth looking at these before going ahead and inviting someone along with you to share your day's hunting.

When I lived in Wales I had perhaps a wider choice of places to hunt than is available in southern England where I now live. In some areas where I had permission to shoot, it was possible to walk all day through beautiful mountainous scenery and not see anyone else. In the event of an accident, a companion would have perhaps been a life saver, as it could take days to find an injured person in some of the remote areas in which I hunted. For the same reason, it is always a good idea to let someone know roughly where you are going when you embark upon a hunt.

Many people find it difficult to hunt without an accompanying friend, although personally I enjoy being alone, content to enjoy quietly the countryside around me.

A dog can be a good companion, but must be carefully trained not to race about uncontrollably, and to keep quiet when the hunt is in progress. Some breeds, such as Labradors, make excellent retrievers, so they have a practical value in the field, but remember that they need a great deal of attention to ensure that they are trained to a good standard. Make sure you have both time and patience before acquiring a dog specifically to take hunting.

Returning to the subject of human companions, check to ensure that the owner of the land is prepared to allow you to take a companion with you. Make sure that whoever goes with you is a responsible individual who will respect the countryside code and not place in jeopardy your future chances of shooting over the land.

I have found that my most successful hunts are carried out when I am alone, partly because I prefer to hunt alone anyway. However, pleasant though it may be to have one or even more companions, unless you can work as a carefully co-ordinated team, you will find that the temptation to speak may be too much. If there are two of you, the chances of a giveaway cough or sneeze are doubled; two people make twice as much noise as one, and it does not require an expert in mathematics to realise that the chances of success are diminished in direct proportion to the number of individuals in the party.

❑ Conservation

Should you be fortunate enough to have your own tract of land over which to shoot, or to have permission to shoot regularly over one particular piece of land, a great responsibility falls upon you. Hunters must be conservationists, land managers and wildlife experts all in one, conscious of which species of animals and birds inhabit the land over which they shoot, and concerned for the welfare of those species.

If that sounds a contradiction in terms let me assure you that it is not so. The indiscriminate destruction of wildlife lowers the moral esteem of anyone who engages in it, and that even applies to verminous species to some degree, since it is not for man to determine the balance of nature.

Occasionally, the balance does become upset, usually due to the activities of man. Pesticides can reduce the number of birds of prey, so allowing some of their natural prey to increase beyond normal numbers. Farmers' crops may be devastated and action may be essential. It is then that the skilled hunter with the appropriate airgun may show his worth and enjoy good sport at the same time.

Obviously, over-shooting an area will denude it of stock eventually, and even if the much maligned rat is the quarry, the simple fact is that once you have shot all the rats, assuming that were possible, which is unlikely, there will be none left to hunt.

On farmland, stock moves in naturally to replenish an area depleted by over-zealous hunting, but the process can take years. Be sensible and husband the resources carefully, giving thought to the future and having respect for wildlife.

❑ Identifying Quarry

Hunters tend to become wildlife experts as a matter of course, since they come into contact with nature at first hand, and need to be able to identify clearly their quarry beyond doubt before squeezing the trigger.

To the inexperienced, the greedy, destructive wood pigeon can look much like a domestic racing pigeon or one of the rarer dove species when partly concealed among leafy branches. The hare, a game animal, can resemble the rabbit when only the long ears are showing above the grass. Acquire an illustrated field guide and study it carefully before hunting, to make sure that you are clear in your own mind exactly what you are hunting and, perhaps more importantly, what you could possibly mistake it for in the field under hunting conditions. Remember, the effect of the pellet is final; you cannot bring it back and start again, so if in doubt, do not shoot.

❏ Accuracy

When you hunt, be sure that you can be certain of a head shot for a clean kill. Nothing less is acceptable. That means shooting at a sensible range; there really is no fixed 'effective range' for an air rifle, in spite of what some manufacturers might lead you to believe. Range depends upon many different factors, including type of gun and its condition, type of pellet used, effect of wind on the pellet, temperature, lubrication, accuracy of the gun, and so on.

Accuracy is far more important than power in any application, and no less so in hunting, although sufficient power is naturally a consideration. The most powerful airgun in the world is useless unless it is accurate enough to hit the target at exactly the point you intend.

If you have a large collection of airguns and tend to use them all, the chances are that you will never become fully proficient with any of them, so pick the one that will do the job and which is not going to be too heavy.

* **Pellets**

Match just one type of proven pellet with the gun and stick to that combination, because different pellets vary in their behaviour and often need slight sighting adjustment to take account of this. Any such adjustment is better made on the target range, where the results can be clearly seen and evaluated, than during a hunt, where any error could lead to unnecessary suffering.

* Sights

Open sights are acceptable for hunting provided that your shooting is of a reasonable standard, but it is generally accepted that a good quality telescopic sight is better, since it facilitates greater accuracy over longer ranges and also permits shooting in lower light levels than would be possible using open sights.

A word of warning, though: a telescopic sight will not necessarily help you to be a better shot. The standard of your shooting will still only be as good as the amount of practice you put in, so do not fit a telescopic sight with the idea that you will suddenly automatically begin to shoot like a top, world-class champion marksman. If you do, you may end up disappointed. Still, a telescope can certainly enable your natural skill to be exploited to its best effect, and to that end they are well worth fitting.

A good telescopic sight is a valuable accessory for the hunter.

It is a fact that young people often shoot to an exceptionally high standard, with or without a telescopic sight, perhaps because they have more time available to practise. If you keep practising, your skill with an airgun will continue to improve.

Do not allow a telescopic sight to encourage you to take shots at excessive range when hunting. The limitations which apply to your particular airgun regarding inherent accuracy and velocity still apply when a telescope is in use; the only real difference is in the shooter's perception of range.

When buying a telescopic sight to be used for hunting, which is, in fact, its primary function, aim for quality, and avoid the cheaper 4 x 15 and 4 x 20 types. These have an inadequate field of view for hunting, and will certainly make the whole process of sighting a considerable strain under field conditions. A good 4 x 32 or 4 x 40, or similar, from a well-known manufacturer will prove to be the best investment.

When putting aside money for a telescopic sight do remember that the mounts usually have to be bought separately. You should check that the mounts you buy will fit your particular airgun, especially if it is one of the lesser known makes or models.

There are many useful types of sight available (see Chapter 5 on accessories), some suitable for hunting, others less so, and some which are totally unsuitable. Seek advice before buying any type of sight other than the conventional sort already mentioned. When you have actually bought a suitable sight remember to test it thoroughly on the target range before venturing out on a hunt.

* Safety

One of the greatest areas of concern regarding hunting is that of safety. Each year there are accidents resulting in injury or death through the disregard for basic safety rules when hunting, so I make no excuse for mentioning safety again. Although many of the accidents relate to the use, or misuse, of shotguns, the principles involved are exactly the same and should be applied when hunting with airguns, which can be just as lethal as shotguns if misused.

It is not enough to assume that because you are shooting on your own land, or on land over which you have exclusive permission to shoot, that nobody else will venture there. Children in particular have a habit of investigating potential new play areas with great enthusiasm and disregard for the possible consequences, and a hunter who is totally engrossed in stalking may not see them enter the field of fire. Avoid shooting through bushes or shrubbery at low levels unless you are sure there is nobody behind, beyond your field of view. Quite often the sight or sound of someone hunting will attract youngsters who want to see what is going on. It goes without saying that you should stop shooting under these circumstances, although there is unlikely to be anything for you to shoot at anyway, since everything for miles around will have headed for cover at the first sign of approaching children.

Stay well clear of public walkways when hunting, and avoid shooting across routes taken by the public, since this is not only illegal but is highly dangerous.

❏ First Aid

Hopefully, by observing these simple rules you will avoid injuring anyone. You may expect when you hunt to collect a variety of scratches, cuts and bruises yourself, from lying in awkward places and from worming your way through undergrowth. To avoid any wounds becoming infected it is worth carrying a small tin containing basic first aid necessities: some plasters, antiseptic cream, cotton wool, a small bandage and so on.

Like many other pursuits, you gain from hunting what you put into it, and if your approach is very casual and you trust to that fickle commodity, luck, you may not be too successful. You must be prepared to crawl around in muddy ditches, lie patiently for an hour or more, and generally get yourself dirty and crumpled to achieve success. In my experience, luck plays a very small part indeed, and those who work the hardest at what they do invariably make their own success.

Chapter 4

Mechanics of the Matter

One of the pleasures of airgun shooting as a pastime lies not just in the shooting itself but in the preparation for the shooting. The same is, of course, true for many other hobbies and pursuits: fishing, sailing, metal detecting, and so on.

A word of warning: uninformed tinkering can lead to accidents involving serious injury. It should be clearly understood, *before* any attempt to dismantle an airgun is made, that spring powered air weapons have their mainspring under a certain amount of compression when the gun is not even cocked. These springs are strongly made, and hold a considerable amount of stored energy. The amount of this energy depends upon the type of gun. In some cases it is just enough to prevent an uncocked airgun from rattling, as it would with a loose spring. In others, the stored energy is very considerable, as the mainspring is under a fair amount of tension, the sudden release of which can be disastrous.

Airgun mainsprings can and do cause severe injury, and are quite capable of removing an eye, all in a fraction of an unguarded moment. When you are working on your gun adopt suitable precautions to protect yourself from similar injury.

❑ **Dismantling your Airgun**

Many shooters are content to confine their attentions to careful polishing of the stock, occasional oiling of the action, and perhaps a little mild customising on the outside of the gun if they have the necessary skill. This sort of limited work can be every bit as satisfying in its own way as a total overhaul of an airgun, and one always seems to shoot better with a well prepared gun.

Mechanics of the Matter

Yet it must be accepted that many of us regard airguns as exciting parcels, which must be quickly opened to view the contents. We enjoy the challenge of carefully dismantling a factory assembled weapon with a view to transmitting the same loving care to the inside of the airgun that we lavish on the outside – the parts that are on view to the world.

Sometimes we are stimulated purely by curiosity and a genuine desire to know how the gun works. More often, it is likely that we hope to improve in some way upon the factory produced article; to make an airgun more powerful; to make it smoother and more pleasurable to use; to improve upon a poor trigger mechanism; or perhaps to eliminate some other feature which we regard as undesirable and to introduce features which we would prefer to see.

It is not the purpose of this book to delve deeply into tuning procedures and stripping-down processes relating to specific makes of airgun, or to attempt to analyse the research which has been carried out in recent years in the area of airgun mechanisms and their function and improvement. These aspects have been adequately covered in several other excellent publications. My aim is to give the newcomer an insight into what to expect and what to avoid when working on airgun mechanisms.

Uninformed tinkering is not only dangerous but can also be very expensive. Modern air weapons may seem quite rugged and sturdy, but they are precision instruments like fine clocks or electronic equipment, and should be treated as such.

Start by obtaining as much information as possible about the airgun you propose to work on. Many manufacturers supply a data sheet with their products, giving a blown-up diagram of the various components, together with a spare parts list. These can help you to understand something about the way the gun works, and give some guidance to any special problems which may be encountered. Makers rarely provide much more than this. They prefer to advise owners to take their guns to a qualified gunsmith for maintenance. In fact, many gunsmiths derive much of their work from the failed attempts of an owner to repair or service his own gun.

The monthly airgun magazines are a good source of detailed information on the maintenance of specific weapons, and sooner or later all the more popular airguns come under scrutiny. The writer who carries out the work on behalf of the magazine will report on any problems encountered in the work, so that others attempting to do the same job will be forewarned, and thus able to avoid any expensive or dangerous pitfalls. There are other books, too, as I have mentioned, which delve in some detail into the stripping down and reassembly of various air weapons.

❏ Some Misconceptions

It is a popular misconception among beginners to airgunning that in a spring powered air rifle or pistol the replacement of the original mainspring with a more powerful spring will result in a big increase in power. I recall, as a youngster, sawing up assorted springs and experimenting with different combinations and lengths of spring in an effort to achieve greater power. I did sometimes manage to produce a fair increase in power, but just as often that improvement would be accompanied by a considerable loss of accuracy as the gun jumped about wildly on discharge. Sometimes there would even be a loss of power, as other components fought a losing battle against the characteristics of a mainspring which was never designed for that particular gun.

Experiments have been made in enlarging the transfer port on several airguns. This is the small hole, or tunnel, through which the compressed air travels from the cylinder to the pellet in the breech. Again, it was found that the characteristics of each gun were different, and although in some cases there was a power increase, in others there was a power loss, as the optimum size of the transfer port was exceeded. Guns modified in this way could easily be rendered as little more than scrap, making these experiments very costly indeed. Avoid uninformed experimentation unless you have a lot of money to throw away.

❏ Friction and Lubrication

Any mechanical device with moving parts, be it an engine, a bicycle, or an airgun, is subject to friction. In simple terms, this is a phenomenon which causes contacting surfaces to try to stick together, rather than slide easily one against the other.

Mechanics of the Matter

Friction generates heat and accelerates wear. Some things, like brakes and clutches in cars, actually depend upon friction to operate. Some trigger mechanisms in guns, also, depend on a certain amount of friction to ensure that they work safely.

When it comes to metal-to-metal contact, though, friction is generally an enemy rather than a friend, and basic tuning has much to do with reducing friction on the internal mating surfaces of an airgun. This can be achieved in a number of ways, as follows.

Friction can be defeated by separating the mating metal surfaces with a lubricant. Traditionally, the lubricant has always been a type of oil or grease, and this has the dual purpose of defeating friction and at the same time reducing wear on the moving parts. In recent years, solid lubricants and silicone-based lubricants have become more popular in the field of airgun maintenance. Moly lubricants, based on slippery molybdenum compounds, have been used in the automotive industry for years, and the success of their application in airguns led to their fairly wide use by the mid to late 1970s, along with other space-age lubricants such as PTFE, which had previously found domestic service as a non-stick coating for saucepans and frying pans.

The so-called solid lubricants are carried in a carrier fluid which may be designed to evaporate once the lubricant is in place, or the carrier may itself be a lubricant, either a mineral oil or a silicone-based lubricant which will help to retain lubrication qualities if the film of solid lubricant should break down. Modern lubricants are often very specialised, that is to say they have been developed to do one particular job, and may not be appropriate in another application. A lubricant which is ideal for a piston and cylinder assembly on an airgun may, therefore, be totally unsuited to a trigger mechanism. It could even cause damage if used in the wrong place. For this reason, and because few of us have specialised knowledge in the field of lubrication, it is important to follow manufacturers' guidance when using any lubricants.

❏ Tuning

How well the moving parts of an airgun operate in conjunction with one another depends not just upon lubrication. The better quality airguns are manufactured to exacting tolerances, and can be expected to perform well. However, even on these guns there may be some room for improvement. Cheaper guns are likely to vary in quality from one gun to the next on the same model, and there is scope for considerable improvements to be made by tuning.

* **Piston and cylinder**

The fit of a piston in a cylinder is critical, since if it is too tight it will not move freely and will thus restrict the available power, whereas if it is too loose a fit, or inaccurately machined, air may leak past the piston seal, again reducing available power. Work in this area is intended to ensure that the piston has as slippery a fit in the cylinder as possible, without being too loose. Peering into an airgun cylinder will often reveal scoring and unevenness on the cylinder walls, and this can be removed with *very mild* abrasives, and finished off to a high polish using a lightly abrasive metal polish cream. Metal-to-metal contact points between the piston and the cylinder should also be highly polished, and any attempts to rush this sort of work by using coarse abrasives will be doomed to failure. More damage is likely to be caused than will be eliminated. If you are short on patience, do not even attempt to start this sort of tuning work.

There is a school of thought which recommends 'glaze busting' the cylinder before reassembly. This process, commonly used in engine renovation work, involves very lightly scoring the cylinder walls by cross-hatching. A light abrasive paper may be used.

The idea is that the surfaces of the piston assembly and the cylinder will bed together effectively, and that the scoring will hold tiny amounts of lubricant which would otherwise be carried away by the piston.

The process should only be used where the piston uses a metal piston ring; a leather washer may be damaged by the process and would not benefit from it anyway. Nylon piston seals carry lubricant away rather than holding it like a leather washer, so some tuners believe that glaze-busting is beneficial in holding lubricant in these cases. I am personally a little uneasy about this, so I use the process only where metal rings are fitted.

Any work carried out on the internal parts of an airgun must be done amid scrupulous cleanliness. Large supplies of clean rag, preferably cut from an old sheet, are very useful, and if abrasives have been used, no matter how fine, every trace of these must be removed using a solvent cleaner, such as methylated spirit, before re-assembly of the various parts. Failure to do so will simply mean that the abrasives continue to do their work even after the gun has been reassembled. While this may well be seen as the lazy man's way to tune an airgun, once the working surfaces are all smoothed down and bedded in, the abrasive will continue to work, accelerating wear to an alarming degree and shortening the life of the gun.

❏ Special Tools

Preparation is the key to any work on the mechanical parts of an airgun and, having read available information on the gun which you intend working on, the next stage is to ensure that you are fully equipped to do the job. Occasionally, special tools may be needed, such as a steel drift to tap out securing pins, but some tools may be easily made or adapted from existing ones. Drill bits of the appropriate diameter are useful for drifting out pins, but care should be taken as bits are brittle and snap easily.

A set of good quality screwdrivers, including Phillips and electrical types, will be a mainstay of your toolkit. Many airguns can, in fact, be stripped down using little more than a single screwdriver. It is important that your screwdrivers are of good quality, as you are less likely to damage stubborn screws than you would with cheap tools. You may find that an impact screwdriver set, which gives added leverage by a smart tap with a small hammer or mallet may be a worthwhile buy, as some screw fittings, notably on the German weapons, can be difficult to remove without damage.

A good workbench with a vice that has soft jaws is another essential, and it should be remembered that an airgun cylinder should be treated gently or it can easily be damaged by a too enthusiastic application of the vice. A cloth and wooden insert should protect the gun when it is being held in the vice, because the steel is very easily marked, and blueing does not need excessive encouragement to come off.

Pliers, a set of Allen keys, especially the small sizes, and some spanners will cover most needs. A few fine files and an oilstone will not go amiss, either. A Mole wrench can be very useful as an extra pair of hands on occasions. However, it should be remembered that this tool, although very useful at times, is the classic 'butcher's' tool, and can wreak havoc on the metalwork of your shiny airgun, so save it for emergencies.

Should you intend to make the stripping down of spring powered airguns a regular occurrence, I would advise you to make up a spring clamp, or have one made for you. As previously mentioned, airgun mainsprings are under a certain amount of tension as fitted, and this tension is released by removal of the cylinder end cap, or whatever similar device is fitted. A spring clamp pressurises the spring as the end cap is removed, then slowly releases the pressure, so that the mainspring can be safely removed. It is possible to make do without a spring clamp by placing the cylinder in the suitably protected jaws of a vice and then pushing down firmly on the end cap as it is being removed. A cloth placed over the cap will guard

Piston and mainspring assembly from a pistol.

Mechanics of the Matter

against its loss and give some protection if whatever you are using to remove the cap should slip. The big disadvantage of this method of mainspring removal is that – apart from being potentially dangerous – it is very easy to slip and for the spring to fly out. You have no way of knowing when the cap is going to come off, so you must maintain the pressure all the time. Unless you have worked on that type of gun before, you have no real way of gauging how much tension is on the spring, and on some air rifles it can be considerable.

The safe answer is to build a spring clamp. The requirements for this can be judged by examining the cylinder of the gun and taking appropriate measurements. Some sort of frame with a bolt which can be slowly unscrewed to release spring pressure can easily be devised, or perhaps adapted from an existing clamp. A good supply of solvent cleaner, lubricants and cleaning cloths will complete the workshop.

I would not advise work to be carried out on pump up guns unless you have successfully done so before. These guns are remarkably trouble free. Provided they are sensibly looked after, occasional lubrication, as directed by the manufacturer, is usually all that is needed. I have seen quite a few ruined by owners' inept workmanship, so if it is working well, my advice is to leave it alone.

Spring powered airguns, in their various guises, present few problems when dismantling. Where a safety catch is fitted, it is normally required to be on 'fire' to enable dismantling to be carried out. Stocks are removed by taking out the fixing screws which are usually quite visible. Watch out for the occasional hidden ones. These may be covered by a plastic insert, or let in from the bottom of the pistol grip, as with BSA guns.

❑ Trigger Mechanisms

It is not generally necessary to dismantle trigger mechanisms when working on piston and cylinder assemblies, unless it is intended to make improvements to the trigger itself. This is a specialised job and should not be undertaken lightly. Some tuners polish the trigger sear to give a smoother trigger release, and the results can be quite a revelation to the shooter afterwards. However, a word of warning: some trigger mechanisms rely upon a certain amount of friction for their effective and safe operation. Elimination of this friction can be dangerous and cause the airgun to discharge spontaneously. The same can occur if adjustable triggers are over-adjusted to give an ultra light let off.

Many trigger mechanisms are totally enclosed, such as the excellent trigger assembly fitted to Weihrauch rifles, and these are best left untouched unless you know exactly what you are doing. These are made to a very high standard, and there is likely to be little or nothing that an average unskilled owner can do to improve upon it. That is not to say that it cannot be improved upon – several specialists have taken up that challenge – but the job is not one for the layman.

❑ Replacing Worn Parts

Air seal washers as fitted to break-barrel air rifles and pistols can be removed with a pin, preferably with a safety pin, and the

Sometimes fixing screws are concealed, as on this BSA Scorpion air pistol.

groove into which the seal is fitted should be carefully scraped out using the same pin. Remains of the old seal, together with any specks of dirt which could prevent the new seal from seating properly, should be removed. The new seal should be fully pushed home and when correctly fitted should stand just proud of the breech face.

Any worn pins or bolts should be replaced, as should worn breech lock fittings, otherwise accuracy will suffer as a result of barrel movement. Damaged screws, bolts or safety catches should be replaced as a matter of course. The mainspring will also need to be replaced in time, and you may be surprised at how much longer the new spring is than the original one. Deterioration takes place over a long period and often goes unnoticed unless the owner makes regular use of the chronoscope. You may decide to invest in an individually produced spring from one of the specialist firms. Some of these are very good indeed and can greatly outlast the original spring. Should

Piston detail.
This one uses a synthetic ring in place of the traditional leather washer.

you adopt this course, you may find that the replacement spring in this case is actually shorter than the original. This is not a mistake, it is just that the characteristics of the new spring are different from the original, and it may be made from thicker steel wire, or from wire having a different profile, perhaps square sectioned.

When replacing a mainspring, I coat the whole spring in a moly based grease. This dampens any movement of the spring on dishcharge, makes the gun altogether smoother and really very pleasant to shoot, and eliminates the 'twang' which is the hallmark of many airguns. I use various appropriate moly lubricants when putting piston and cylinder assemblies together, and use a more conventional light oil on trigger mechanisms.

Every gunsmith has his own favourite concoction of lubricants, often mixed up to a jealously guarded formula. The

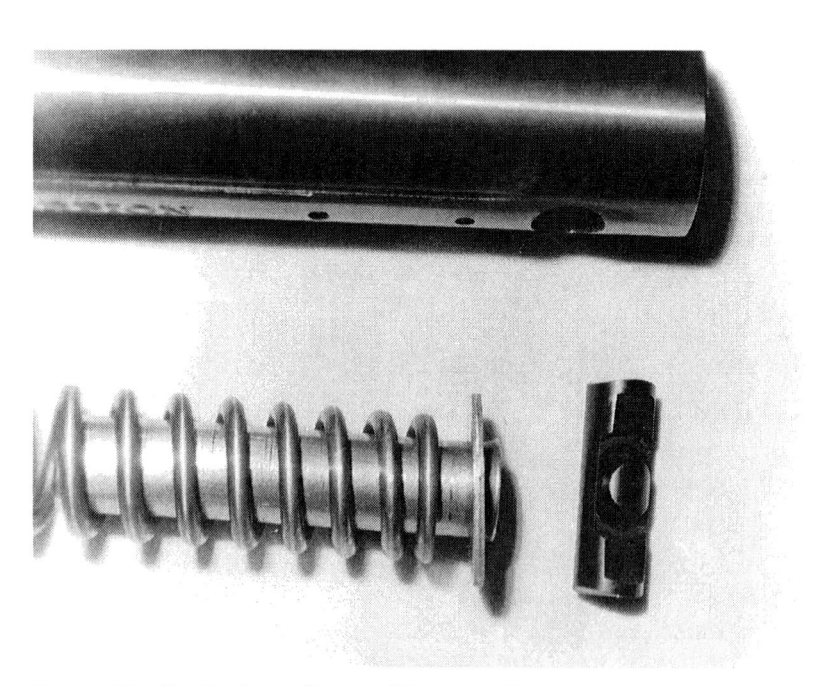

Be methodical when dismantling an airgun.

Mechanics of the Matter

important thing, as previously stressed, is not to overdo lubrication. This can cause as many problems as it cures: detonation, loss of power, fouling of the barrel, etc. Use lubricants sparingly and keep your work spotlessly clean at all times. Just a trace of grit can cause considerable damage if not quickly removed. It eventually becomes ground down to a fine grinding paste, which shortens the life of your gun. After reassembly, a light film of oil or rust inhibitor on all the metal surfaces will help them to remain rust free.

Incidentally, when applying moly lubricants to the cylinder walls of an airgun, the lubricant should be rubbed into the metal, rather than just smeared on. Moly based lubricants have some interesting properties, one of which is that they actually form a kind of bond with the metal, so in this respect they differ greatly from oils and greases.

There can surely be few situations as unsettling as disman-

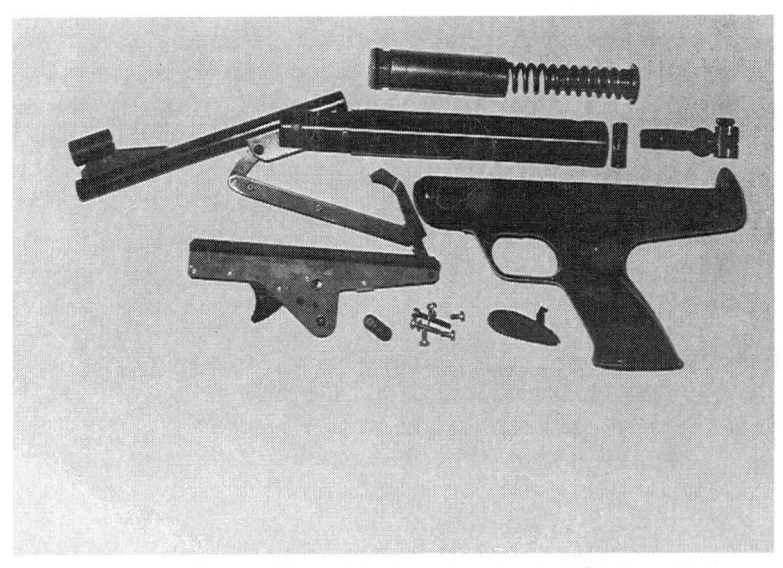

It is important to be methodical when dismantling airguns, as there are many small parts which can easily become lost. Make a note of what goes where, too!

tling an airgun completely, carrying out whatever work is necessary, preparing to reassemble the gun, and then finding that you are left with a heap of screws, bolts, and other components, with no clear idea as to how they should be reassembled. Sometimes after reassembling a gun completely a single solitary little spring or small screw may be left. The gun seems to work all right, yet at the back of your mind you know that the manufacturer would hardly provide that component if it were not needed.

Problems of this kind can be avoided in a number of ways. Before starting work on any job which involves dismantling mechanical parts for the first time, have a pencil and paper handy to detail each step as it is taken. This can be done by listing each stage under a number. For instance, you may write: No. 1: remove three screws holding stock to action. No. 2: put the screws in box A.

This brings us to the second stage of avoiding chaos. Obtain an assortment of containers for holding screws, pins, springs, etc. Old pellet tins are very useful for the purpose, and if you buy some stick-on white labels from the stationers you will be able to number or letter the containers for instant identification. Be systematic at all stages of the operation and you will make life very much easier for yourself. Loose screws lying around on a work bench are easily knocked off and lost, too, and many of these are not easily replaced, having been specially made for their particular purpose. If you place them carefully in containers, the chance of their becoming lost is greatly reduced.

Fortunately, airguns contain relatively few individual parts, so unless you propose to be ambitious and dismantle a complex trigger mechanism, you should not meet with too many problems. Remember though, that even with few component parts, if you spread the work over more than a day it is very easy to forget what goes where. Sometimes you meet a component which can be put on in more than one way, though only one of those ways is actually correct. Should this be the case, you would be wise to mark the component to indicate which way round it should be fitted. Typewriter correction fluid is useful here, and it comes in a convenient little bottle with its own brush.

The amount of work which can be carried out by an owner on

his own gun depends very much upon his individual ability and whether the type of gun lends itself to the relevant degree of home handiwork. Some jobs are best left to a well equipped workshop. It is possible to straighten a bent gun barrel in a home workshop, but this is not a job to be lightly undertaken since it is relatively easy to make the problem worse by putting an additional bend further down the barrel. Any work requiring machining, brazing, or welding is best carried out by someone who has the appropriate equipment and the necessary expertise.

It is relatively easy for an owner to make and fit his own leather washers and air seal washers. I buy old leather belts or handbags for a few pence in jumble sales, and the leather lasts for ages. I also use it to produce useful accessories, such as a holster for a pistol.

Chapter 5

Accessories

Accessories fall broadly into two categories: the items which can actually add to the standard of your shooting, such as telescopic sights, pellet sizers and tuning kits; and items which make no difference at all to your shooting, but which are nevertheless satisfying to possess. The latter group includes pellet holders, plinking targets and polish for the stock of the gun.

Some might argue that even items which have no obvious direct bearing on the performance of the gun or that of the shooter may still improve his shooting by making him more comfortable, thereby improving his concentration. An example would be protective clothing. Someone who has confidence in his own equipment and its reliability will, naturally, perform better than the shooter who is forever having to tighten screws or make adjustments. It really comes down to deciding, firstly, what you would like, and then what you can afford.

Fortunately, as with most pastimes, once the essentials have been purchased, other useful items can be added to the collection in a piecemeal fashion over the years.

❑ Protective Clothing

Arguably, one of the most important accessories, and that which commands a substantial share of the market, is protective clothing. Before buying special clothing, take stock of what your requirements really are, just as you did when choosing a gun. That way you will avoid wasting money on inessentials or unsuitable equipment. If, for instance, your interest is strictly plinking, and you never venture out in wet or very cold weather, there is no need to purchase special clothing: an old anorak will suffice. Perhaps all you need is a hat with a brim to shade your eyes from the sun, and maybe a pair of gloves to keep your hands warm on a chilly day. One of my own best buys was a pair of thermal mitts – open fingered to allow easy handling of fiddly pellets, yet still quite snug on a cold day.

If you intend hunting in all weathers it is worth considering thermal underwear. It can actually improve your shooting by allowing you to concentrate on what you are doing, instead of agonising over the bone- numbing cold seeping relentlessly though your thin clothing.

Camouflage-type outer clothing is fine for hunting, but make sure that it is also waterproof, not just showerproof, and that it has a degree of resistance to thorns and brambles. It should also have a thick lining for added warmth, and ideally this should be removable to avoid discomfort in warm weather. The

There is a very wide range of accessories available.

waxed cotton 'keeper' type coats, with good deep pockets and effective waterproofing are an excellent buy, and are available in shades of green and brown which blend in well with the countryside.

Once you have a good jacket, and perhaps a hat with a peak to keep the sun out of your eyes and flaps to pull down over your ears, you have the main basic clothing. You may then decide whether to add waterproof overtrousers to complete the outfit.

Match shooters can buy a mitt to support the gun, clothing padded in various interesting places, barrel weights, a peaked cap to shade the eyes, ear muffs to eliminate distracting noises, and even special shooting spectacles to help the shooting eye to focus on the sights rather than the target itself.

Footwear is worthy of close consideration, especially for the hunter. During the summer I am always torn between wearing light sports shoes, like trainers, to facilitate quiet, light-footed stalking, and more substantial footwear, such as some form of boot. The type of terrain likely to be encountered will obviously have much to do with the final choice. If the ground is likely to be at all soft and marshy, then a strong pair of waterproof walking boots will prove a useful choice.

Wellingtons are not the best choice when out shooting, unless the terrain really is extremely soggy, because they are uncomfortable to walk in for any distance and give little support to the ankles. If you feel the need to wear wellingtons, invest in a pair of woollen sea-boot stockings to help cushion the boots and absorb perspiration. These extra long, thick socks should also be worn with other types of boot. Remember to allow for their thickness when selecting your boot size.

Tinted glasses are a popular accessory with match shooters, and worth a try if strong light tends to affect your eyes.

❏ Telescopic Sights

Just about the first accessory bought by anyone with an air rifle is a telescopic sight. Perhaps I should clear up a few misconceptions regarding 'scopes before going on to consider what is available. A 'scope will not necessarily improve your shooting; if you shoot poorly with open sights then you will also shoot poorly with a telescopic sight. There is no magic property to a 'scope which will make anyone an instant expert, but used

Accessories

properly it can add a new dimension to your shooting.

Sighting can be a little slower with a 'scope, and the expense is probably not justified for casual plinking sessions, particularly as some 'scopes will not focus down below 4 or 5 metres – the distance at which many back yard plinkers may do much of their shooting.

For hunting, however, a good telescopic sight can make the best of fading light, giving useful extra hunting time. Properly set up, it will give just enough magnification to allow clean head shots on rabbits and other vermin at a sensible range.

Telescopic sights range in price from single figures for a little 4 x 15 or 4 x 20 'scope (which is sometimes supplied with a gun as part of a package deal – usually in mail order catalogues) to treble figures for precision instruments with zoom facilities.

Most confusing to a beginner are the strange numbers identifying the various 'scopes. The first number indicates the magnification – 4 x is about right for airguns – while the second figure identifies the size of the objective lens. The larger this second number, the more light enters the instrument, and the greater the area which can be viewed through the sight.

Resist the temptation to go for high magnification, in the hope that you will be able to shoot individual feathers off wood pigeons at 100 metres. With an excessively high magnification, all that will happen will be that you will spend a very long time just trying to find the target through the 'scope. Even the benefits of a large objective lens will be cancelled out by too great a magnification. When you do eventually pick out the target, it will seem to be jumping around wildly, with every tiny movement you make translating itself into much bigger movements through the instrument.

Avoid the very cheap telescopic sights, and also the expensive, gimmicky 'scopes with lots of interesting, but often unnecessary features. A good make of 4 x 32 or 4 x 40 instrument will prove an effective choice for most eventualities.

❏ Protection for Your Gun

Protect your expensive air rifle with a sturdy, waterproof gun cover. This will help to prevent scratches and scrapes while the weapon is being transported, or while it is in the cupboard at home. Small cases are available for pistols, although you may like to try making your own. Quality is very much related to price with gun covers. A good cover is not cheap, but can be expected to last the life of the gun, and even longer.

❑ Velocity Testing

Those who become deeply involved in airguns as a sport will sooner or later want to be able to test the velocity of their gun, or guns. There are a number of reasons for velocity testing, apart from just being interested in knowing the performance of a particular gun out of curiosity. The performance of a spring air weapon falls off over a period of time. There are several reasons for this: the mainspring becoming tired, air seals beginning to leak, piston washers wearing and allowing air to pass on the compression stroke, and simply general wear. Often a new mainspring and a replacement air seal washer will be all that is needed to restore peak performance.

A gun's performance, like that of a car, can deteriorate so slowly over a long period of time that it is hardly noticeable and some means of measuring the power loss is useful. This is particularly important to the hunter, who relies on an adequate velocity to achieve clean kills.

The muzzle energy output of an airgun must be within the legal limit, and this is often tested at field target events, so an enthusiastic owner, who enjoys working on his own gun, must have the means of velocity testing, both to stay within the law and to avoid disqualification from such events.

* **Chronoscope/chronograph**

An airgun which is inconsistent from shot to shot as regards power is likely to be equally inconsistent as regards accuracy. Correct lubrication can eliminate the problem, but it is vital to know when the difficulty has been solved. To discover this a chronoscope, sometimes called a chronograph, is used.

The chronoscope is an electronic device with two sensors set at a fixed distance apart. When a pellet is fired between the sensors, the instrument measures the time the pellet takes between the two, and from this the velocity can be calculated – either manually, using a conversion factor supplied with the chronoscope or, in the case of a top quality instrument, in the

Accessories

chronoscope itself.

Since chronoscopes cost as much as a good air rifle, the outlay is not really justified unless you have a business dealing in airguns, or have a large personal collection of guns.

* Ballistic pendulum/sledge

A cheaper way of gaining an idea of the velocity of your gun is to use a ballistic pendulum, or a ballistic sledge. With the former, a pellet is fired into a metal cup on the end of a pendulum, which moves a needle on a gauge. The readout can then be used to calculate the velocity.

The ballistic sledge operates similarly, but more directly. Ballistic pendulums and ballistic sledges are accurate enough to give a fair guide, but cannot compare with a chronoscope for consistency. They are dependent upon careful use, and are subject to variations due to friction and temperature fluctuations.

* Ballistic putty

For those looking for a rough guide, ballistic putty is available. This is like plasticine in consistency. Pellets are fired into it, and comparisons made between penetration depths. It has a use as a comparative medium for tests between similar guns which are being tried out at about the same time. The results are subject to considerable variations in consistency, as the putty softens when handled. It does, however, make good plinking targets.

When carrying out velocity testing, be sure to adopt a procedure of firing a number of shots, eliminating any very high or very low readings, then taking an average of those left.

❑ Targets

There are many different types of target available, ranging from conventional competition card targets, to cards depicting various types of vermin. There are purpose-built plinking ranges of steel construction, with re-settable targets and built in pellet traps. Electronic ranges are also available for those looking for something a little special.

❏ Decoys and Camouflage

Hunters are a good market for the accessory manufacturers, and for those who take their hunting seriously, the range of goods available is considerable, since, to a degree, it also takes into account the large number of shotgun users.

Enthusiasts will not just shoot their quarry; they first hide from it in a hide constructed with Ministry of Defence surplus camouflage netting. The quarry is then encouraged into the general area with a specially made call, which guarantees to sound just like the real thing if used skilfully. You can call crows, ducks, and others, but not rabbits as yet, though I am sure the manufacturers are working on it!

If the quarry is wood pigeon or duck, it may be fooled into thinking that it is safe to feed by the sight of what it takes to be

A wide range of camouflage clothing and accessories is available, though it is not necessary to spend a great deal of money.

Accessories

several of its fellows apparently enjoying a hearty meal. These are actually specially made decoys of plastic, wood, fibre glass, or even cardboard. A science has evolved around the question of how decoys should be set up, in which direction and in what attitude. The determined hunter will even put one up a tree if he is hunting pigeons in an effort to simulate the 'lookout', which feeding birds always rely upon to warn them of impending danger.

Having lured the hapless bird, the hunter will then take aim through his electronic red dot sight, or telescopic sight, squeeze the carefully adjusted trigger, and send a cleverly designed two piece hunting pellet on its way to despatch the bird.

If his quarry is a rabbit, the hunter will know that gutting, or paunching, is best done straight away, and for this he uses a carefully honed, multi-purpose survival knife, which is often nearly as expensive as the rifle. He then threads the rabbit onto a game carrier's loop.

It is easy to dismiss camouflaging as a gimmick, but if done properly, it can be staggeringly effective. I bought a camouflage suit at a game fair a few years ago, and used it on an evening rabbit hunt some time later. I was standing motionless next to a sycamore tree, waiting for a rabbit to show, when a buzzard wheeled in and flapped around within literally a foot or so of my head. This was quite an unnerving experience and I thought the bird may have been trying to intimidate me, but it flew to another tree just a few metres away and began preening itself. Clearly it had not seen me.

❏ Tuning Kits

Maintenance should be restricted to occasional oiling of moving joints, and a few drops of moly lubricant introduced to the cylinder from underneath, or from the transfer port. This must be used very sparingly, or, as we have already mentioned, a phenomenon known as dieselling or detonation will occur. Excessive lubricant ignites with a louder than usual crack, and can seriously damage a gun if allowed to happen very often.

If you still prefer to work on your own gun with a view to improving its efficiency and smoothness, you can buy tuning kits which provide the necessary equipment and instructions to enable you to carry out the work yourself.

❏ Silencers

Since the early 1980s, silencers have gained a degree of popularity, with several manufacturers now producing them, usually as a sideline to some other product. Silencers assist in reducing the blast as the pellet leaves the barrel, an effect which is more marked in some guns than others. They can obviously do nothing to reduce mechanical noise, which can be a fair proportion of the overall noise in a spring operated weapon. This mechanical noise can be reduced by use of one of the tuning kits already mentioned.

It stands to reason then that silencers are most effective on guns having a fairly noisy muzzle blast. The improvement on some pump up guns can be quite significant, since they have relatively little mechanical noise on discharge. The improvement is usually more noticeable to a bystander than to the actual shooter. Silencers can have a very small effect upon the accuracy of an airgun, and perhaps on the power, too. This is likely to be due to turbulence, or to the diffusion of the air propelling the pellet. The effect is minimal, however, and some makers claim to have eliminated the problem completely.

❏ Pellets/Sizers

The number of types of pellet on the market is vast. Try them all, but then stick to just one or two types, or the consistency of your shooting may suffer. Lead pellets are easily damaged, and a pellet sizer will ensure the consistent size and shape of each pellet if you have the time to use such a device. Sizers appeal to target shooters, who are more inclined to inspect each pellet closely for the slightest imperfection.

❏ Trigger Shoe

A tiny but useful accessory is a trigger shoe which, as the name implies, fits over the standard trigger to give a greater feeling of control. This in turn can improve accuracy. It is an excellent accessory, and is helpful if your gun does not have an adjustable trigger.

Accessories

❑ Magazines/Books

The number of publications relating to airguns is fairly small at present, but the quality of those on the market is excellent, and they are well researched and informative. The monthly national magazines are a very good way of staying in touch with current trends and prices, and they are worth compiling into a binder for reference purposes. The list of accessories is almost endless, and part of the enjoyment of airgun shooting is in browsing around the local gun shop.

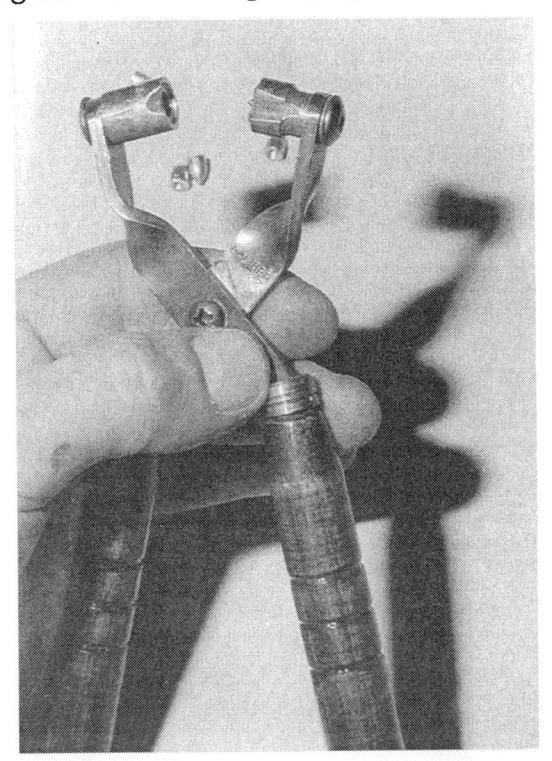

A pellet mould for the manufacture of lead pellets at home.

Chapter 6

Refinishing and Customising

Own an airgun and sooner or later you will probably want to work on it, to improve its appearance or performance. I do not propose to deal in detail with the dismantling of specific airgun mechanisms, but there are a few hints which would-be customisers may find useful.

❑ Repairing and Refinishing the Stock

No matter how well looked after, any gun will eventually collect a share of dents and scratches, and these are probably best ignored until they begin to make the gun unsightly. Dents in wooden gun stocks can be removed quickly by applying a hot iron to a wet cloth placed over the damaged area. The steam encourages the wood to swell, drawing out the impression. In the case of a very large dent, the operation may need repeating a few times. After treatment, be sure to allow the wood to dry thoroughly before refinishing. If the dent is too big or stubborn to respond to this treatment, the only course is to fill it with plastic wood and then to use a darker varnish to hide the inevitable colour variation.

Before carrying out any work on the stock of a gun, you should be aware that the commonest stocks, made from beech wood, are usually given a colour varnish, or even stained, by the manufacturers. This will be apparent if the stock is scratched, since the colour shows through as a lighter shade. It will be obvious that simply touching in damaged areas with clear varnish is not likely to conceal blemishes fully. The answer is to remove the stock from the gun and sand it down completely.

It is usually obvious from a detailed inspection of the gun which screws need to be removed to detach the stock from the action. Watch out for screws fitted from under the pistol grip section; these may be concealed beneath a removable plastic plate. Once the stock is off the gun, all the varnish should be carefully removed by sanding with a medium grade glass-paper. Avoid using an extremely coarse grade in an effort to speed up the job as this can cause deep scoring, which in turn can be difficult and time-consuming to remove.

Be prepared to spend a long time, several evenings, if necessary, in preparing the stock for refinishing. After the main varnish has been removed, use successively finer grades of glass-paper to achieve a very smooth finish, rubbing out scratches as you go along. Ensure that your hands are clean and free from grease while doing this work, or you may find that the new varnish may not take properly. For the same reason, be sure that every last layer of the old varnish is removed, in case it is incompatible with the new. This may result in a wrinkling effect.

I suggest you use polyurethane for the new varnish, as it is very resistant to scratching and various solvents which may accidentally find their way on to the gun. This type of finish can be bought with an incorporated stain if you do not want to use a clear finish.

* **Varnishing**

Using a very clean, dust-free brush, put on a single, thin coat, and leave in a warm place overnight. When the varnish is completely dry, rub the stock with a very fine grade 'wet or dry' paper, used slightly wet, until the surface of the stock feels smooth. Although it will seem that you have undone all your work by removing the varnish, what you have actually done is to fill the grain of the wood, in preparation for the finishing coats. Five or six of these finishing coats will then be needed, rubbing down very lightly between each one to avoid a build-up of dust or unevenness on the surface. Keep each coat as thin as possible, or unsightly runs and streaks could appear. If you are a hunter and want to avoid the gun being too shiny, use an 'eggshell' or matt final coat. If using a gloss finish, the final coat should be deep, smooth, and free from blemishes. If there are specks of dust on the surface, wait for a few days for the varnish to harden fully, then burnish the surface, using an abrasive metal polish, working on a tiny area at a time. Finish off with a wax polish.

* **Inlaying**

An idea which you may like to try if your are re-varnishing the stock is to buy a piece of thin dowelling from the local do-it-yourself store; a piece about the thickness of a pencil will do. The stock of your gun can be drilled using a suitable sized bit to a depth of a few millimetres to take a section of dowelling. This should be stuck in using a resin woodworking adhesive, leaving a small amount of dowelling protruding. After an hour or two to allow the adhesive to dry, the protruding dowelling can be trimmed off flush with the surface, using a sharp wood chisel, and then sanded. If you stain the dowelling an appropriate contrasting colour before use, when the whole thing is varnished the inlaid dowelling will stand out as a feature of the stock. With a little imagination, sections of dowelling can be arranged into geometric patterns, or even your initials if you prefer. The whole job is cheap, and quite easy to do, but test on an old piece of wood first in case your drill is not quite the right size – it must be spot on.

This process involving dowelling is a technique known as inlaying and, if you have the confidence and the ability, you can expand the idea by making designs out of thin pieces of contrasting coloured wood. Trace round these on to the stock of the gun, and carefully cut out the exact shape using a very sharp craft knife. Scrape out the area to a depth of a millimetre or so, using a sharp chisel, and stick in the shaped piece of wood. Once the adhesive has dried, as with the dowelling, the proud surface of the wood can then be planed and sanded down to the level of the rest of the stock.

You may be able to buy small pieces of mother-of-pearl from larger music shops. This material is used extensively by musical instrument makers for inlaying, and can look very attractive when set in a dark wood background. Handle it carefully though, as it is extremely brittle and snaps easily.

Perhaps you do not feel confident enough to inlay your gun stock, but would still like it to look a bit different. The Royal Society for the Protection of Birds occasionally market rub-down transfers depicting different bird species, and these can

Refinishing and Customising

look very striking on a gun stock. A coat of clear varnish will stop them washing away at the first hint of rain, and also lend protection against abrasion.

Why not paint motifs or animal silhouettes on to the stock? Many stationers and fancy goods shops stock stencils with a variety of interesting patterns which could be used for the purpose. Test whatever paint you intend to use on a small area first to ensure compatibility with the existing finish. Degrease the stock carefully before painting, ensuring that there are no residues of wax polish left, then lightly sand the area to be painted to ensure a good key for the paint. As with all other jobs of this type, practise first on something other than your treasured gun stock, then, when your technique is satisfactory, apply your new skill to the stock itself.

* Replacing pistol grips

Pistol shooters often find that the standard butt grips supplied with the pistol are usually less than ideal, and would like to change them. Some of the more expensive air pistols have modified grips available as optional extras, but it is not too difficult to make your own if you wish, or if modified grips are not available. Many types of close-grained hardwood are suitable for the purpose, and a timber merchant should be able to find you a small offcut of walnut, mahogany, beech, maple or something equally suitable.

The usual deficiency with standard grips is that they are 'universal' – designed to suit almost everyone reasonably well, but almost nobody very well. Pack thin layers of well worked, warm plasticine around the original butt grips, then squeeze the grips firmly until the plasticine takes on the shape of your shooting hand and the pistol feels comfortable to you. The new grips can be carefully worked using chisels and perhaps sanding discs in an electric drill, shaping the grips gradually to conform to the plasticine pattern. If you are in your early teens you may need to do the job again in a year or two as you grow.

If you feel adventurous, you could try making butt grips from papier maché. It needs a lot of patience, but this medium is actually extremely strong and malleable. A craft book from the local library will help you. I have just finished constructing a guitar case from this material, and the result is strong, light, and attractive. Instead of painting the finished case, I simply gave it a coat of clear varnish, leaving the strips of newspaper which formed the maché as a decorative feature. It is a real attention grabber. Papier maché, when dry, can be drilled, sawed and sanded, just like wood.

* Blueing the metal parts of the gun

Damaged metal parts are a little more difficult to put right. Although fairly resistant to scratching, the factory blueing on a steel barrel can wear away eventually, and this could accelerate the onslaught of rust. Again, there are no real short cuts, and once the gun becomes too unsightly for your peace of mind, the only answer is to re-blue it. In the factory, blueing is applied using heat, but cold gun blue cream can be bought from local gun dealers. This does a very acceptable job without the need for heat or messy chemicals. Take care when using gun blue though, as it is corrosive and poisonous.

With the stock removed, use a very fine 'wet or dry' paper (used wet) or else fine wire wool to remove the existing blue. It will pay to try the blue on a very small corner first, to ensure that it works on your particular gun. Some weapons have a finish which will not accept blue. Once the surface has been cleaned back to bare metal, and any rust has been removed, the whole part to be blued should be de-greased using a solvent cleaner. Methylated spirit does a good job, but use a clean, lint-free cloth to remove any powdery deposits before commencing blueing. As with any repair job, time spent in meticulous preparation will be repaid by the quality of the final finish.

Detailed instructions are provided with cold gun blue, and these should be carefully followed. The cream is applied to a small area at a time, and care should be taken to avoid going over the same area twice, as this can cause colour variation. If the colour needs to be deeper, the whole area can be covered again once the first coating has been applied. If the preparation work was properly done the final finish should be as good, perhaps better than, the original.

Some guns have an epoxy-type black finish which can be difficult to remove, and the metal underneath may not take a blue, so try a small area first. You might need to resort to a metal scraper to remove this type of finish, but try not to score

Refinishing and Customising

the metal itself.

Customising really is a field of study on its own. There is something deeply satisfying about creating a gun which stands out from the crowd and looks really special. Many individuals, however, do not feel that they have the necessary skills to enable them to carry out customising work, yet many small jobs can be done without the need for specialised equipment or facilities. The main point I think is to build up confidence gradually by working on scrap materials. Do not try to be too ambitious all at once, such as attempting to create elegant scrolls and hunting scenes on the woodwork. Often the simple designs and ideas are the best.

Once you have worked on a few basic customising projects, such as making new butt grips for a pistol, or revarnishing a stock, you will find that you begin to develop the self-confidence to tackle larger projects. Patience is really the key to success in any worthwhile customising project, since any attempt to hurry the job is sure to spoil the end result. I must confess that I am not always too good at following my own advice, and occasionally I am up burning the midnight oil in an effort to complete a job which I have been looking forward to showing off at a field target event the next day.

The best way to tackle a large customising job is to think of it as a collection of individual smaller tasks – it can be a little daunting to look at a rough-hewn chunk of wood and try to visualise it as a sleek custom gun stock. Take it stage by stage, and it will not seem so intimidating.

❏ Building a Custom Stock

Let us look at the stages involved in, say, building a complete new custom stock for an air rifle, complete with inlay and varnish.

Good planning is essential to any project, and customising is no exception to this rule. Decide first exactly what you want from a new stock. Perhaps you have seen a custom stock in a gun shop or at a competition and decided it would look smart on your own gun. Remember that a custom stock should feel more comfortable in use than the original stock, and the gun should be quick to come on target. They are not designed just to look attractive, but have a positive function, too. They should fit the requirements of the individual shooter better than the mass-produced article.

Try some different modified stocks if possible before you start building. Shooters at field target events are often only too pleased to have other enthusiasts admire their guns, and will usually allow you to heft the gun and feel the difference between the modified version and the standard article. The difference can be quite considerable, and can make a pleasant surprise to anyone who has not tried one before. Make sure you are fully happy with the style of stock and are going to be able to live with the design before starting work.

* **Selecting design**

Ensure also that the design of the custom stock you have in mind is appropriate to your own gun. I once built a custom stock for a BSA Mercury, using maple, an expensive, fine-figured white timber, and modelled the stock on one I had seen on another make of air rifle. After about two months of spare

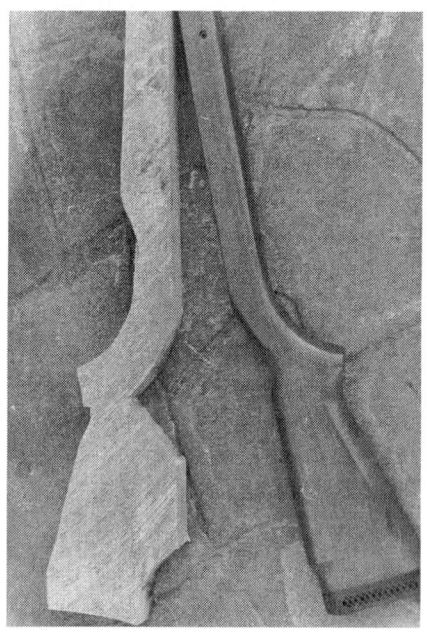

The beginning of a custom stock, seen alongside the standard stock.

Refinishing and Customising

time work, culminating in the installation of dark rosewood inlay and ten coats of clear varnish, the stock cracked at the pistol grip the second time I used it on the gun. I gave the remains of the stock to a wood carver friend of mine to use to make small items rather than waste the fine timber. I had made the mistake of applying the wrong type of stock design to my gun. The pistol grip area was too narrow to take the strain of the cocking action of the air rifle on the large screw which lets in through the base of the pistol grip on the Mercury. It may well be, too, that there was an invisible flaw in the timber which I used, and perhaps the angle of the pistol grip was too sharp to provide the needed strength.

Avoid making the same mistake by looking carefully at custom designs which have been applied to your particular make and model of gun. Follow the basic designs adding your own individual ideas. Of course, if you have one of the more unusual models of air rifle you may be very much on your own and need to experiment to achieve results. Remember the mistake which I made, and hopefully it will help you to avoid possible pitfalls

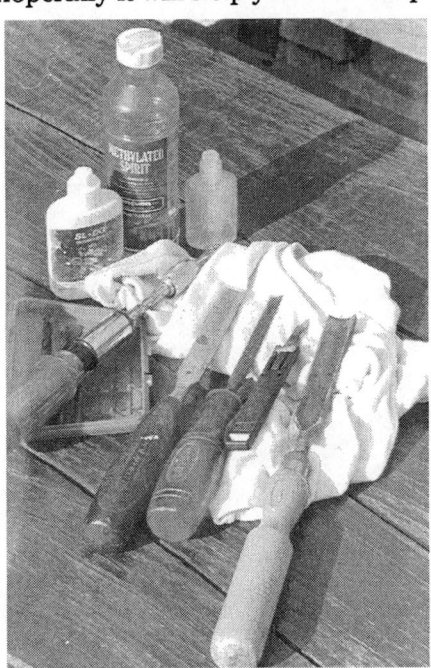

Few tools are needed to carry out basic work on an airgun.

at the outset.

* **Obtaining the wood**

The wood for a stock can be obtained from gunsmiths and occasionally from stalls at game and country fairs. Incidentally, these types of events are often a useful source of both materials and ideas, attracting as they do specialists from all over the country. Watch out for dates of fairs in your local county magazine or in the airgun magazines.

Of the available timbers, English walnut is the most popular, and justly so, being beautifully figured and a real delight to look at, but it is expensive. Other hardwoods can be effective, though not all are suitable. Mahogany and similar timbers are used quite often, but personally I find this type of timber tends to dent a little more easily than some. Rosewood is beautiful but splits rather too readily. It is best for inlaying, especially with a lighter coloured timber such as maple.

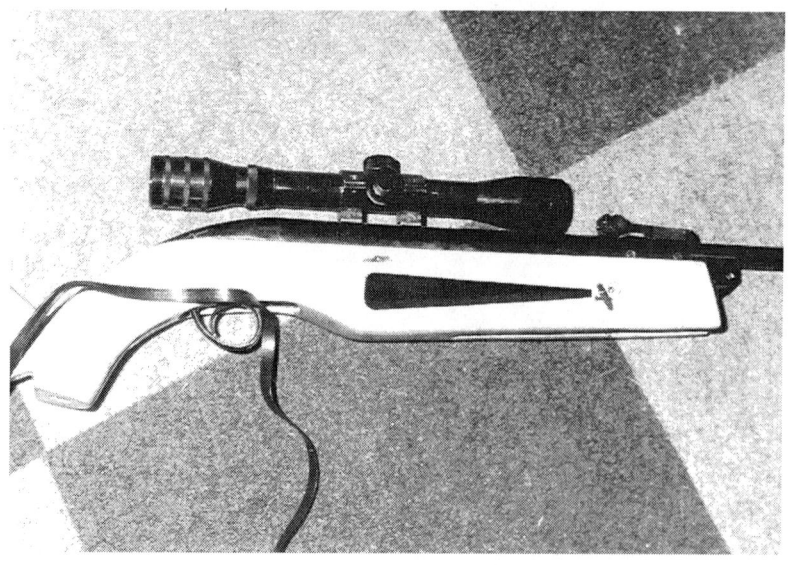

A maple custom stock with rosewood inlay.

Refinishing and Customising

Timber can be ordered from a specialist hardwood supplier; many timber yards deal almost solely in softwoods, and either have difficulty in obtaining hardwoods or are simply reluctant to order the small quantities required by customers.

* **Cutting and shaping**

Your air rifle will have an existing stock which has cut into it various grooves, holes, notches and so on to take the action. These must be faithfully reproduced on the new stock, so they need to be carefully measured and recorded. An effective way of doing this is to use tracing paper to transfer the general shape of the cut-outs to the new stock. The depths of these recesses will vary, too, so care should be taken when recording the information not to miss any detail.

First plane down the timber to give a reasonably smooth surface for marking out, then rough out the overall shape with a pencil, allowing plenty of room for final shaping and for any small cutting errors you might make. Saw out the rough shape, having first checked that the pencil markings are in the right place and that you have the correct dimensions before proceeding.

The top of the stock into which the action fits needs to be flat and square, so that the inletting may be accurately cut to take the cylinder of the rifle. This is the area to work on first using a good quality smoothing plane. Hold the stock in a carpenter's vice or Workmate to keep it steady as you work; protect the wood from the jaws of the vice with cardboard.

The actual inletting, unless you have access to expensive power equipment for specialist woodworking, will need to be carried out using hand chisels of appropriate sizes and probably a gouge. A gouge is simply a type of chisel with a rounded rather than a flat blade. Depending on the make of the air rifle being worked on, it will probably be required to cut the channel in which the cylinder rests.

A mallet will be needed for use with the chisels, too. The work will involve much testing for the fit of the cylinder in between chiselling, and you should avoid cutting too much wood off in one go – it is much easier to remove wood than to put it back. If you do take too much wood off, however, you can repair small damaged areas using a proprietary wood filler such as Plastic

Wood, or you can make up a filler of your own to match the wood, using fine sawdust from the wood itself, mixed with a suitable clear or semi-clear adhesive. I have done this myself very effectively, but plenty of practice is needed to ensure an accurate match. It is far better not to take off too much wood in the first place.

One thing you will notice if you have to fill overcut areas is that these will often be a different shade, usually darker, when varnished. What looks like a good match at the time may be less so when the work is fully completed. Test first, complete with varnish, on off-cuts to be safe.

Once the action sits neatly into the new stock, any holes needed for securing screws can be drilled. Having done that, remove the action and continue shaping the wood towards the finish.

A tool called a spoke shave (a type of two-handed plane) is useful for initial shaping of a stock. Chisels and planes may also be used. At the risk of offending traditionalists in woodworking, I am going to suggest an alternative, and faster, way of achieving the final shape of your custom stock: use an electric sander, or drill with a sanding attachment (rotary), and fit a medium grade sanding disc. Use this to shape the stock carefully. Do not be tempted to use a coarser grade of disc to speed up the process, since the faster cut may cause you to remove too much wood, and the coarser discs can leave deep scoring. You may then remove too much wood while trying to get rid of the scoring. Change to a fine grade sanding disc at an early stage to avoid these problems.

The eventual finishing needs to be done by hand. This is probably the most time-consuming part of the whole process and must not be skimped. Any abrasions will show up much more prominently when the varnish is applied, even though such defects may not be noticeable at the sanding stage. A good idea is to sit down and watch television or listen to the radio as you work – it makes the job seem less arduous.

* **Inlaying**

Select whatever material you have decided to use for inlaying, be it contrasting hardwood, mother of pearl, plastic or whatever. If you decide to be adventurous and utilise unusual

Refinishing and Customising

materials for inlaying, be careful that whatever you use will not shrink or crack when installed, spoiling the final finish.

Install the inlay in the manner described earlier in this chapter, levelling the surface flush with the stock as soon as the adhesive has dried. Once you have had practice at inlaying (it is essential to practise on scrap materials before touching your valuable stock), you may feel like having a go at creating some more ambitious shapes to inlay: animals, birds, geometric designs, etc. Modelling drills and very small wood carving tools are useful here, and you can let your imagination run riot.

You are no doubt wondering how to cut around a complex shape in detail to inlay it. What you actually do is to cut around the main shape of the inlay, as accurately as possible, but ignoring any holes and detail cuts. Inlay the piece and when set, sand down flush with the stock as before. The remaining detail is then filled using a filler which matches exactly the wood from which the stock is made. This can be made up or bought, as

These rosewood pistol grips are inlaid with mother-of pearl. The saw cuts in the pearl are filled with shellac.

described earlier.

If you are using a dark timber for the stock, a substance called orange shellac, which can be ordered through chemists, may be used to do the filling. Shellac comes in flakes, and is brittle, breaking up easily with rough handling. It is used in the manufacture of traditional French polish.

Heat up the tip of an old screwdriver for about thirty seconds or so over a gas flame. Place a flake of shellac on the inlay, then apply the heated screwdriver to the shellac, which will instantly melt and fill the holes. Sand down as before.

Heated shellac can be mixed with small quantities of sawdust for a more accurate colour match, but it is unsuitable for light coloured timbers, being of a darkish brown itself.

If you prefer to use transfers rather than inlay, these can be applied after the first coats of varnish have been allowed to dry. The final coats of varnish then protect the transfer and stop it from rubbing off.

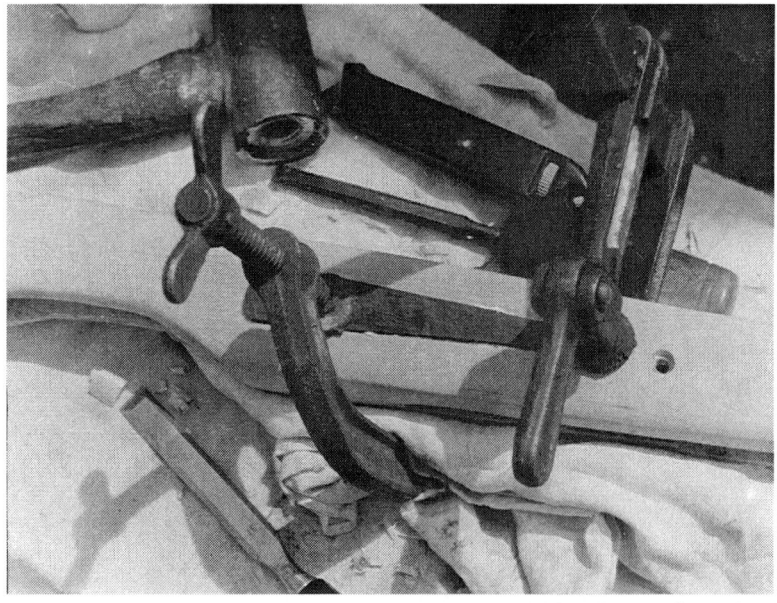

A contrasting piece of wood makes an attractive inlay. When the adhesive has set, plane and sand the inlay flush with the stock.

* **Finishing and varnishing**

When the final sanding is completed, the grain of the timber needs to be sealed to ensure a smooth, clear result. Before applying any sort of finish, ensure that your hands are clean, then pass them over every part of the stock. This will effectively remove any dust which might otherwise spoil the final result. There are grain sealers which can be used, but some of these impart a degree of colour or irregular marking which is undesirable when a clear finish is used.

I usually apply a single coat of varnish. Polyurethane is very durable, and there is a choice between a non-reflective silk finish or a high gloss. When this first coat has dried thoroughly I rub it down using a finishing grade of 'wet or dry' paper. As the name implies, the abrasive paper can be used wet or dry, though it does last longer and finishes more smoothly if it is used wet. This means, though, that the work must be carefully washed and then thoroughly dried before applying the next coat of varnish.

The first coat of varnish effectively fills the grain, then a succession of coats can be built up to give the desired depth of finish, rubbing down lightly to remove dust between coats. This is known as 'flatting'. The final coat should be left for a week to harden fully, and then can, if required, be treated with rubbing compound, available from car accessory suppliers. It is a mildly abrasive cream which is rubbed into a section of the stock at a time, then rubbed off with a clean cloth, having removed a microscopic surface layer of varnish, together hopefully with any surface ripples or other irregularities. Be careful not to rub too hard when using rubbing compound or you will cut right through to the wood. For this reason, it is worthwhile to finish with at least six coats of varnish, or even more. This gives you a greater depth of finish to work with, but avoid allowing surface irregularities to build up in the hope of removing them at the rubbing compound stage. It should only be necessary to remove a very fine film with the compound. The compound can then be washed off and the stock buffed with a clean dry cloth.

Next use a mildly abrasive metal polish to remove any blooming left by the rubbing compound, and after removing all traces of these materials a fine wax polish can be applied. If you have opted for a silk or matt finish, the final polishing stages can be omitted. If you have no experience of these processes, practise on scrap materials first before touching your prized custom stock.

Finish is very much dependent upon good preparation and time spent at the sanding stage will be well repaid, as will the use of a good quality brush when varnishing. When applying a clear varnish do not use a brush that has previously been used for paint, no matter how well cleaned. However, a well-used, softened brush is better than a new brush, which is best avoided unless it is of sable or similar soft hair. Even then it is likely to shed a few hairs at first.

Part of the attraction of customising is that you can use your own imagination widely and can be innovative. I think there is something of the adventurer in all of us, so customising is sure of a great future.

Index

Agreements (for use of land) 29
Airgun magazines 9, 29, 41, 63, 72
Air seal (see *Seals*)

Blueing 68
Breech lock 49

Calibre, choice of 32, 33
Chronoscope 12, 15, 49, 58, 59
Conditions of entry 14
Conservation 23, 35
Customising 64, 69, 78
Cylinder 43, 44, 46, 50, 73

Decoy pigeons 22
Decoys 60
Dieselling 11, 51, 61

Elevation 5
Entry fee 9

Fieldcraft 24, 30
First aid 39

Glasses 56
Gun case/cover 57, 58

Hidden target shoot 20, 22
Hides 30

Injury 2, 34, 38, 40
Inlaying 66, 71, 74-76

Lubricants/lubrication 11, 15, 16, 36, 42, 43, 44, 47, 50, 51, 58, 61

Mainspring (see *Spring*)

Marshall (see *Range marshall*)
Moly lubricants (see *Lubricants*)
Muzzle energy/velocity 10, 12, 15, 28, 58, 59

Novelty range 19

Open sights (see *Sights*)

Pellets, choice of, 33, 36
Pellet moulds 63
Pistols 20, 53, 57, 65, 67, 69, 71, 75
Piston 43, 44, 50, 58
Pneumatics & pump-ups 47, 62
Port (see *Transfer port*)
Power (see *Muzzle energy*)

Range Marshall, Range Officer 14, 16, 17, 20
Red dot sights (see *Sights, Red dot*)

Seals 6, 44, 48, 49, 53, 58
Shooting rights (see *Agreements*)
Sights, Aperture 5
    Diopter (see *Sights, Aperture*)
    Open 37
    Red dot 61
    Telescopic 5, 6, 11, 13, 20, 37, 38, 54, 56, 57, 61
Silencers 62
Sizers, sizing 54, 62
Snap shooting 21
Spring 40, 42, 46, 47, 49, 50, 52, 58, 62

Tap (see *Loading tap*)
Telescopic sights (see *Sights, Telescopic*)
Trajectory 1, 12, 38
Transfer port 42, 61

Trigger shoe 62
Tuning 43, 44, 54, 61
Turbulence 62

Vermin range 18

Windage 5

Zeroing 5, 6, 10, 11, 15, 16

Other airgun books from Peter Andrew

Airgun Shooting – An Introduction
by Les Herridge

This is the companion volume to Les Herridge's 'The Airgun Shooting Handbook'. Contents include law and safety; choosing an airgun; where to shoot; using the gun; ballistics; and competitive airgun shooting.

Vermin Control with the Air Rifle
by Jim Tyler

This book is the first serious treatise on the subject from a universally recognised authority. Contents include the definition of vermin; selection of a suitable air rifle; sighting system and pellet; pellet trajectory; methods and tactics.

Airgun Sport
by Jim Tyler

Jim's second book delves deeply into all aspects of the sport of airgun shooting. An excellent read for both beginner and experienced airgun shooter.

Airgun Field Target Shooting
by Les Herridge and Ian Law

This authoritative book provides the reader with a comprehensive insight into this fast growing sport.